Not Today, Negativity!

Welcome to the first day of your UNLIMITED LIFE!

Positively yours,

Dr Dreda

Praise for
Not Today, Negativity!

"In her moving and powerful memoir, Dr. Oneeka Williams guides us in divine moments of deep and needed self-reflection about fear and encourages our courageous examination of those fears using empathetic words and poignant personal narratives. *Not Today, Negativity* is a fascinating, conversational read due to Dr. Williams' skillful integration of humorous, memorable and spellbinding life stories. This book provides relatable lessons and quotable gems of transformative wisdom that lead us to designing more empowered, positive and joy filled lives."

—Natalie A. Cort, Ph.D.
Associate Professor, Clinical Psychology Dept, William James College Co-Director, Center for Multicultural & Global Mental Health Director, Black Mental Health Graduate Academy

"Dr. Williams captivates her readers with riveting stories about her life, her work to incorporate the 5 Habits of Positivity in her daily routine, and the many challenges she faces along the way. I could not put the book down, and found myself enthralled with every personal incident dealing with illness, difficult colleagues, infertility and much more. This book is a must read for anyone who wants to take control of their emotions and live a happier, more positive life."

—Lisa Jones M.P.P
General Manager, Childrens's Programming, WGBH-Boston

"Sage advice intertwined with riveting stories. Dr. Oneeka Williams guides us on a journey to becoming our better selves with clever acronyms, deeply personal life lessons and enthusiastic encouragement."

—Monique Rainford MD, OB/Gyn
Former Chief of Obstetrics and Gynecology, Yale Health

"Dr. Oneeka Williams has penned a fabulous, intimate memoir! She shares herself daringly and I was captivated by her vulnerability in a way that I have never experienced before. Her journey has blessed me immensely and the stories and tools have graciously equipped me to soar into my unlimited! This book will be a game changer for a whole lot of people!"

—Debra Wright, MD, MPH
Gynecologist/Lifestyle Medicine,

"Dr. Williams' stories are so powerful. Her reserves of positivity are astounding."

—Pamela A. Mason, Ed.D.
Director, Language and Literacy Program,
Senior Lecturer on Education, Harvard School of Education

"An enthralling presentation of life experiences…emphasizing that each of us have a powerful story to tell if only we have the courage to reveal it. In this book, Dr. Oneeka Williams has drilled down to her core, and bravely revealed her power of positivity. She invites, encourages and empowers you to do the same."

—Hubert S. Williams
Caribbean Journalist, Dad

"Dr. Oneeka Williams has given us a perpetual gift in this compendium—*Not Today Negativity!* She has masterfully woven her stories and the stories of others into a beautiful tapestry leaving you wanting more—and there is more! I have re-read chapters and received new revelation, perspective and hope! Be prepared to be challenged, be prepared to be wowed and be prepared to unearth your unlimited life!"

—Janita K Burke
Consultant, Lawyer

NOT TODAY, NEGATIVITY!

5 Habits of Positivity to Cope, Hope, and Be Well in Tough Times

DR. ONEEKA WILLIAMS

ISBN 978-0-9983045-5-7 (Paperback)
ISBN 978-0-9983045-6-4 (ePub)

Library of Congress Cataloging-in-Publication Data is available through the Library of Congress

Publisher: Dr. Dee Dee Dynamo Books
897 Washington St, #600496
Newtonville, MA 02640
info@drdeedeedynamo.com

Printed in the United States of America

Dedicated to all of our angels who brought love, light, joy, hope, laughter, and inspiration while on Earth and now hover protectively over my family and me. We feel your presence, and you live in our hearts forever.

Acknowledgments

The journey to this book would not have been possible without the strong, broad shoulders on which I stand. I humbly acknowledge my ancestors, teachers, and mentors.

My deepest gratitude to my family who has loved me, cared for me, encouraged me, believed in me, guided me, prayed for me, cooked for me, celebrated me: maternal grandparents, Doris and John B; paternal grandmother, Audrey; great aunts Enid, Sybil, and Thora; Uncles Cyril, Boyo, and Benjy; godparents Olivia, Rufus, Norma, Dennis, Rickey, and Dolly; Aunts Barbara, Jean, and Walterine; the myriad of cousins and god-sisters in Barbados, Bermuda, Georgia, Guyana, London, Maryland, New Jersey, New York; Family in Love Queen Bea, Poppa Charles, and all the Anderson/Johnson families.

I pay special tribute to my parents, Hubert and Eugenie, whose sacrifice, love, investment, commitment, role modeling, and support nurture me to this very day.

My deep affection and appreciation to my bestie Paula, my phenomenal sister-friends, book club sisters, prayer partners, church family, Alpha Kappa Alpha Sorority sisters, The ConstructHers, Jack & Jill moms, Links sisters, and Mocha sister docs who have encouraged, read, given feedback, edited, and cheered me along the way. I am very thankful to my layout team and editor.

Words cannot fully express the love and gratitude that I feel for my special home team, who have been a part of my dream and championed this journey with their unconditional love and support: my amazing husband, Charles; my twin, Hubert Jr, his wife, Evandra, and her mom, Maria; my wonderful son Mark; and my nephews, Lucas, and Jacob (the threesome known as the "Brozins").

To my Positivity Posse Tribe, I thank you for riding with me!

Most of all, I thank God for His goodness and provision during this entire process.

AUTHOR'S NOTE

The Urology Stories do not represent a single patient but are a compilation of many different scenarios that capture common urologic entities. All names and any potentially identifying information are fictitious. Names of non-family members within my stories have been changed to maintain privacy.

Contents

INTRODUCTION

"And we know that ALL things
work together
for good to those who are called
according to His purpose."

—ROMANS 8:28

> *"Owning our story can be hard but not nearly as difficult as spending our lives running from it. . . . Only when we are brave enough to explore the darkness will we discover the infinite power of our light."*
>
> **—BRENE BROWN**

HOW MANY STORIES DO YOU keep hidden? What would you do if you knew your stories had the power to heal yourself and others? You would probably start shouting at the top of your lungs to anyone who would listen. I'm beginning my shout today! How about you? Sharing my stories with you has been such a healing journey. I believe you will also find the healing path in your stories by journeying with me through mine. Even in the toughest of times, you will learn to craft your own stories in a way that heals hearts, restores bodies and minds, elevates you above your circumstances and empowers you to take action.

I truly believe I was born on the Island of Positivity! Does that mean that I have been shielded from negativity? No! Despite the number of times that life's problems have steamrolled me, with the help of God's amazing grace, I have picked myself up, dusted myself off, squared my shoulders, assumed a defiant stance, sprinkled in some spunk, and said, "Not today!" Not today, fear! Not today, worry! Not today, anxiety! Not today, insecurity! Not today, defeat! Not today, negativity! Negativity is like a villain hell-bent on stealing every good thing in our lives, but we can fight back and protect our birthright.

We are often held captive by our problems because we think that problems and negativity are partners. They are not! We know problems are a part of life, but when we allow them to marry negativity, they become a formidable couple that can come at us so ferociously that we buckle under the onslaught.

How many of you have had days when you have...

- Felt so overwhelmed by problems and circumstances that you crawled back into bed and shut down?

- Felt exhausted, afraid, and alone?

- Felt so diminished and devalued by toxic relationships or environments that you became physically ill?

- Looked at a world where the odds seemed stacked against you and felt discouraged about the future?

- Felt like you were working hard, but the harder you worked, the more stuck you became?

- Wondered how you could find the positives when the world seemed to be drowning in a sea of negatives?

I've had those days! Are you shocked? A successful, Harvard-educated urologic surgeon and award-winning author with everything going for her, has felt this way too? How can that be? Let me tell you. Training and working as a female surgeon in a male-dominated world meant that I had my fair share of those days. No one is exempt from tough times. It's part of being human. What do we do during those times? Do we throw up our hands in defeat? Or, do we get out of bed and declare with some attitude and some spunk, "Not today, negativity, not today!?"

How did you feel when the United States took a collective pause in March 2020 because of COVID-19? I imagine positivity was not high on your list of emotions. Disruption, fear, insecurity, feeling overwhelmed, uncertain, and worried most likely dominated. Negativity seized the opportunity to prey upon us. I am sure that many of you have dealt with small COVID-19-like moments in your life. Times when it seemed as if your life was turned upside down. I have had many, but the most difficult were the ten-year infertility journey, multiple pregnancy losses, postpartum hypertension, dealing with toxic male surgeons, and navigating a healthcare system that failed me even though I was an insider.

The COVID-19 pandemic has been like nothing we have ever encountered. The crash coincided for all of us, even though our individual experiences may differ. For parents, the responsibilities of managing the educational, emotional, mental, and physical needs of our children rose exponentially, leaving many of us feeling overwhelmed. Some of us were ripped apart by the deep pain of lives lost. The image of a White police officer kneeling on the neck of a Black man in callous disregard for his life was seared into our consciousness. It broke my heart to know that some women and children suffered more abuse and violence during the pandemic, and the disproportionately lethal impact of COVID-19 on Black and Brown people left me cringing.

It was as if a high-wattage spotlight illuminated the negativity that has fueled centuries of injustice, discrimination, racism, gender inequity, and misogyny, which destroy our bodies and minds. Isn't it mindboggling to think that the very pandemic that has created so much hardship has also generated a confluence of circumstances that has ignited the possibilities of Positivity Power within us? This drives us toward hope in action as we push to obliterate the reign of terror inflicted by centuries of limited thinking and negativity. How can we harness that power and apply it across all areas of our lives?

If you admit that limited thinking and negativity have left you feeling discouraged and disheartened, and you want to move beyond just coping and treading water to stay afloat, this book is for you. If you desire to do more than survive, but you want to hope and thrive with flair and spunk, this book is for you. Whether you are a Black woman, a mom, an immigrant, a woman in medicine, a woman who experienced infertility, a woman who has had to wrestle the healthcare system, or a woman who has been disrespected and treated unfairly in the workplace and you want to approach your challenges with hope, this book is for you. If you would like to train your children not to feel defeated when tough times roll in, but to develop a process that builds resilience, this book is for you. If you simply want to think more positively so that you can be healthier, this book is for you. According to the National Science Foundation, the average person has 12,000 to 80,000 thoughts per day, and 80 percent are negative! So, we are all in a full-on battle with negativity. You can be a positivity catalyst that introduces this life-changing process to any environment.

This is a deeply personal book. It speaks to the range of my experiences and reaches across labels. I pray it will cultivate compassion and understanding. As I share myself with you, I'm willing to bet that if you are a woman between the ages of 20 and 80, you will see yourself in some of my experiences. As I bring you on my journey to discover the 5 Habits of Positivity (HOP), I hope it will inspire you to apply them in your life and provide some reliable artillery to defend against negativity's attacks.

A Crash Course in Limited Thinking

I stepped off the plane from Barbados at age 18, college-bound, and received a crash course on how tough it is to be Black, female, and an immigrant in the United States of America. Add the surgeon to the mix (later), and I was really in a bind! In all these areas, I felt "otherness," as if I lacked value and worth and didn't belong. It didn't take long for my new reality to slap me in the face. Three days after I first set foot on my predominantly white college campus, the pre-med advisor told me I should plan to return to the Caribbean for medical school because I would not get into an American one. She saw me as "other."

How many of you have had similar experiences that left you scratching your head? Was it my skin color? My braided hair? My gender? My accent? The color of my dress? Was it a socioeconomic issue? A religious issue? A cultural issue? She made some significant assumptions about me based on her biases, and I continue to encounter many of these roadblocks today. How could I possibly be positive when I rode on a tsunami of history, deeply embedded traditions and practices, stereotypes, and negative expectations? Little did I know these would be the micro and macro aggressions that would accumulate over time and form the basis for the chronic stress that would put me at risk for the health challenges that I have experienced.

Years later, I attended urologic surgical meetings, viewing the sea of alabaster heads, smooth and shimmering like pearls strung around the room. For a brief but interminable moment, my mind would say, "No one else looks like you." I was one of the 0.001 percent of physicians who are Black female urologists. I had chosen this specialty on the first day of my ambulatory surgery Veteran Affairs Hospital rotation as a third-year medical student. My first patient in the outpatient urology clinic was an elderly man who had the misfortune of having a life-threatening scrotal infection. The urologists saved his life by removing his scrotum and implanting his testes into his thighs. They worked with him in a way that restored his hope and subsequently reconstructed his scrotum. As crazy as it may sound, I instantly felt, "Wow, this is what I want to do!" Fortified by my sense of calling, I would scan the room full of White bald heads at those meetings, and my heart would whisper, "You belong here." I would resist the urge to turn around and run and remember that I was "different," not "other." I was supposed to be there. I could not allow limited thinking and negativity to win. "Not today, imposter syndrome! Not today!"

"Weathered" but Not Defeated

Being on high alert all the time, waiting to repel the daggers of discrimination, gender bias, microaggressions, and disrespect is exhausting and destructive. I had never heard the term "weathering" in medical school. The term was coined in 1992 when Arline T. Geronimus conducted a study of National and Nutrition Data and proposed that Black people experience early health deterioration because of the cumulative impact of repeated experience with social or economic adversity or political marginalization. The level of education or socioeconomic status is not protective. I certainly never considered that the chronic stress of living and training as a Black woman in America to pursue my highest calling of being a surgeon would place my mind and body at significant risk. I learned firsthand, experiencing almost every adverse outcome.

✓ Higher rate of infant mortality
✓ Higher rate of premature delivery
✓ Higher risk of C-section
✓ Higher rate of postpartum complications

✓ Higher rate of physicians not listening and believing my symptoms

✓ Higher rate of substandard care

✓ Higher risk of chronic illness

✓ Higher likelihood of discriminatory treatment in the workplace

✓ Higher likelihood of unequal pay

✓ Higher risk of being racially profiled

I was STRESSED, and there were days when I did not want to get out of bed.

Yet, it was the smackdown of coming to America that pushed me onto the Scaffold of Positivity that positions me to be your Positivity Catalyst. I could either choose to stay discouraged, helpless, frustrated, and depressed or hold up my hand and declare, "Not today!" I grabbed hold of Positivity Promises that life is 10 percent what happens to you and 90 percent how you respond to it. I held on and launched my Habits of Positivity.

Even at the most tenuous of times, I learned:

- You can strike me down, but as Maya Angelou said, "Like dust, I'll RISE."

- When I thought I was not enough, I was connected to an unlimited source; therefore, I was unlimited and more than enough!

- I can choose to establish an internal Island of Positivity, and that process is critical for my emotional, mental, and physical health.

- How to convert "other" to "different" and embrace all the power and richness of differences.

- That we make assumptions about each other based on the external, but as a surgeon, I know that when we peel back the layers, we are more alike than different.

- I had a gift of weaving my science knowledge, passion for healing, and zest for teaching with my creativity, optimism, and personal story.

- How to put my hand up, roll my eyes, snap my neck, and say, "Not today, negativity! Not today!"

If I could do it, so can you, and I'm going to show you how! As a female surgeon, my day was sometimes punctuated by subtle digs and blatant acts of disrespect that would drive the blood pounding to my head. I needed to learn ways to actively diffuse that intense physiologic response.

There is power in awareness.

Imagine 5 Habits of Positivity as armor, to not only protect your health but also to add pep to your step and confidence that drives your hand up to negativity, indifference, envy, feelings of inadequacy, self-doubt, and judgment. A shield that helps you to not only cope, but also hope and believe that:

- There is always a solution; I just have to work to find it. **(HOP #1)**

- I can convert a limit into an opportunity. **(HOP #2)**

- I'm going to hold on to the positives and discard the negatives. **(HOP #3)**

- My purpose is uniquely designated and linked to how I can help someone. **(HOP #4)**

- I can always find reasons to be thankful and believe that there are no limits. **(HOP #5)**

I wasn't born reciting these Habits of Positivity. As I looked back on my journey to becoming a urologic surgeon, award-winning author, and Positivity Catalyst, I realized I was using the Habits without knowing. That was likely why I didn't remain discouraged and disenchanted. When I dissected each of the situations that I describe in this book—and so many more—common coping themes emerged. Those themes all revolved around finding some vestige of positivity, pushing myself out of bed, squaring my shoulders, and being intentional in saying "Not today" to negativity.

And why does this matter? Because we have to take part in building a kinder and more caring, inclusive, equitable, respectful, and healthy world, not only for ourselves but also for our children. We are only as strong as our weakest links. As long as we allow negativity's offspring (hate, discrimination, racism, misogyny, xenophobia, bullying, all forms of abuse) to grow, they will continue to weaken our society, prevent real social justice, erode innovation and progress, and hinder economic development. We have to eliminate the places where limited thinking and negativity thrive. We can do this by creating Positivity Scaffolds one habit at a time. It starts with you! When you create your Positivity Scaffold, you can build everything in your home upon it. The effects ripple out like a pebble dropped into a lake to touch your family, coworkers, community, city, state, country, and the world. The more conscious you become of practicing these Habits of Positivity, the more you will connect to your unlimited inner power.

Positive Parenting Matters

Where does positivity come from? It is half nature and half nurture. My parents were sticklers for education and held my twin brother and me to the same standards. At age 13, I encountered quite a dilemma when I decided that I wanted to study physics, a prerequisite for medicine. My brother's all-boys school offered physics as a subject, but my all-girls school did not. The limited thinking and negativity of gender bias struck, and my parents rolled up their sleeves for a fight. I don't think the school was ready for my mom when she jumped into the fray! As a young girl, she was a gifted and highly motivated student, and she was the first in her family to get a scholarship to attend one of Guyana's top high schools. She wanted to study medicine, but her family could not afford to send her to medical school. Instead, she pursued her love of science and became a passionate educator. She would not allow the dream of having a doctor in the family be deferred for yet another generation. My mom said, "Not today," to limiting girls! The following academic year, I marched into my brother's single-sex school as the first girl to enroll in his high school class of all boys.

I saw the power of my parents, believing that there had to be a solution (HOP #1). Their advocacy converted the limit of lack of access for me into an opportunity, not just for me but for other girls (HOP #2). I never remember them communicating about the difficulties of arriving at this unorthodox solution, and as such, I didn't have much anxiety about the decision. Instead, they focused on the positives of the experience (HOP #3). They set the tone as I navigated the uncharted territory of being a rose among thorns. I realize now that I believed in myself because my parents and teachers believed in me. They created my first Positivity Scaffold. My transformation started with them the same way your children's transformation begins with you.

How the 5 Habits of Positivity Can Help You

This is a book of HOPE — "Acting with the expectation of a solution." As our world swirls around us and limited thinking and negativity seem to gain strength, we can fight back! We won't allow negativity to gnaw away at our physiology, destroy our families, prey on our children, erode our communities, and steal our emotional, mental and physical health. Do you want to be well and resist negativity's influence? Do you want to chart a healing journey of positivity, one habit at a time? If the answer is, "Yes," this book is for you!

My journey has been one of self-discovery, and I'm so excited for you to start your journey with me. We will use Positivity Scaffolds, which can take any form. The possibilities are as endless as your imagination. I have distilled the practice into five simple habits, and as we explore them one at a time, they will create the scaffold upon which you will layer your experiences.

Too often, we try to bite off more than we can chew, and the process becomes overwhelming. Applying the Habits of Positivity to your life one habit at a time allows for manageable bite-size chunks until you achieve mastery. If you practice consistently, they will become second nature and a mindset. You will learn a lot, elevate above your circumstances and begin to feel more empowered every day. As you model and share with those in your life, it will position them to transform their thinking and exercise these habits every day, especially during challenging times. A highly effective strategy for change is visualization. Jack Canfield, the co-author of *Chicken Soup for the Soul*, says visualization activates your creative subconscious, programs your brain, activates the law of attraction and builds your internal motivation. This book integrates creativity and self-expression to generate tangible tools to establish the visual framework to support you on your journey. I have created everyday scaffolds like the Inner Superhero, Treasure Chest,

Life Fabric, Joy Tank, Life Pendulum, Life Scales, Life Slingshot, Positivity Champion, Positivity Window, Life Staircase, and the Island of Positivity as fun ways to incorporate the daily practice of the 5 Habits of Positivity.

The more you practice, the more automatic the Habits of Positivity will become, and the more your unlimited nature will be revealed. I can't wait to show you! By practicing the 5 Habits of Positivity, you understand that you have internal S.U.P.E.R. powers established before you were born. Your journey of self-discovery is to find what is already there. You are born with a laden Treasure Chest and a Joy Tank that is overflowing.

Our stories create a rich Life Fabric—our life swings like a Pendulum. We gaze through our Positivity Windows into the Unlimited Sky of Favor. We affect the world like Slingshots and climb our Staircases of Faith. Our life is like a dynamic balance Scale. We can all call forth our Positivity Champion and Inner Superheroes and, we can all create our Island of Positivity wherever we are. As I share my stories with you, I have added exercises and daily practices that help you implement and embed the 5 Habits of Positivity as a way of life.

If you do the work of building onto your scaffolds one habit at a time, you will experience a mindset shift by the end of this book. You will put your hand up with intention whenever one of those negativity invaders pops into your head. Imagine the power of connecting to the unlimited version of yourself by simply deactivating negativity! Launch your Habits of Positivity with confidence. You will be well-positioned to cope, hope, and secure your *emotional, mental, and physical well-being during tough times.* Let's stamp out negativity and hop into hope, love, favor, peace, grace, faith, joy, forgiveness, power, and courage.

Sometimes setting an intention of what you are going to do can feel overwhelming and out of reach. Start with setting the intention of what you will not do. Think of a closet cluttered and overflowing with old, moldy clothes. Unless you clear out the closet, there will be no room for fresh, clean clothing. Worse yet, the mold will spread to your clean clothing if you pile them on top of the contaminated clothing. When you set the intention to not allow negativity to occupy your prime mental real estate and then consciously remove negativity, what you are doing is creating space for positivity. For that reason, this book starts with the declaration, "Not today, negativity"! I am Dr. Oneeka Williams—your storyteller, healer, teacher and, positivity catalyst! Join me on this journey of how we can put our hands up to negativity and build positivity, one habit at a time?

Let's HOP to it!

HOP TO IT!

HOP is the acronym for the Habits of Positivity, but it also conjures up action in two dimensions — jumping upward and moving forward. To hop has an association of gayety and joy and is usually a light-hearted movement. We can achieve a hop with varying degrees of energy, and hops can be taken at any pace, fast or slow, big or small. Hops require intentionality and pauses. Whenever you see HOP in this book, it is an invitation and reminder to actively use your Habits of Positivity to move you toward the desired outcomes of courage, hope, love, joy, peace, forgiveness, grace, power, favor, and faith.

How To Use This Book

As you read the stories, reflect on where you see yourself in them. Use the Positivity Pauses as an opportunity to put negativity on pause. The pauses will help you to redefine, recharge, and reset before you resume and can be as short as 3 minutes. Take at least ten deep breaths at the beginning of the pause and use the time to do an uplifting self-care activity from the categories described in Chapter 2 or reflect on a theme in any of the chapters. Try to take at least 5 Positivity Pauses daily and use your journal to chronicle your Positivity Practices and transformation.

CHAPTER 1

The 5 Habits of Positivity (HOP)

"For He SHALL give His angels charge over you, to keep you in ALL your ways . . ."

—PSALM 91:11

"Challenges make you discover things about yourself that you never really knew. They're what make the instrument stretch—what makes you go beyond the norm."

—CICELY TYSON

HAVE YOU EVER HEARD YOUR grandmother say, "It is well with my soul"? This is the "wellness" that grounds us in peace and an inner knowing that there is a belief that forms the foundation for building towards emotional, mental and physical health despite the vicissitudes of life. My insights come from my struggles, triumphs and transformation, and from being a surgeon for the past 20 years. I have had the privilege of helping patients navigate their medical and surgical needs and have learned the value of perspective on patient experience and outcomes. I have found that assisting patients to view their situations through a process of positivity allows them to cope and be hopeful, even in the face of distressing diagnoses. My goal is to share what I have learned so that you will apply this powerful approach in your life to help you cope, grab ahold of life circumstances, and wave the flag of hope even in the most difficult situations.

Positive emotions add to us like helium in a hot-air balloon, lifting us into the flight of well-being, which gives us an aerial perspective that creates balance and hope. Negative emotions take huge bites out of our joy, faith, hope, and peace. They will swallow them whole if given the opportunity. Negative feelings are like squatters who move into your home uninvited and refuse to leave. It is essential to recognize them and understand how and why they weaseled their way into your consciousness. Every time you kick them out, they somehow make their way back in! Acknowledge how they make you feel, but don't allow them to make your life their permanent home. Why the push to build on positivity? Because there is healing in positivity. Positive people are less likely to feel helpless. Well-being is tied to positive emotions: positive people perform better in sports, are more productive at work, are less stressed, have fewer heart attacks, and live longer. People who are positive live from a place of abundance rather than lack. Positive people are healthier.

The 5 Habits of Positivity can become the scaffold upon which you apply your life experiences, enabling you to identify light and positivity even in your most austere moments. This requires structure, time, and practice. Like any construction project, building occurs one block at a time. You can't start a construction project without the following:

- A goal as to why you are constructing the building— what is the need?
- An architectural drawing (This book helps to lay out the plan and pour the foundation.)
- The scaffold/framework built one habit at a time
- The materials
- The workers

The same is true for positivity. Even if you cannot visualize the final form despite the drawings, focus on laying your circumstances onto the scaffold one piece at a time. Follow the blueprint, and the final result will always lead to positivity. Think of baking a cake. Mixing the ingredients and following the recipe may not initially lead to a perfect cake, but it's a cake nonetheless, and with practice the cake improves. It's not always easy, but it will be well worth it if you do the hard work.

This book shows you how to build your scaffold one HOP at a time and layer your situations onto it. Eventually, you will become so adept at layering your situations onto the entire scaffold that you will see all the Habits of Positivity unfolding in your circumstances—no matter how challenging. Whether you are filtering your situations through the Positivity Filter of your Treasure Chest or launching the Habits of Positivity from your Life Slingshot, the analogies will create a tangible way to apply the habits. As I share my stories, understand that I am using multiple habits simultaneously. You can look for how all the Habits of Positivity show up. However, I will highlight one habit within each chapter for ease of organization, understanding, and practice. As you think about your situations, which may or may not mirror some of mine, you can identify the threads of the other habits within my stories and apply them to yours.

Habit of Positivity (HOP) #1

There is always a solution; work to find it! Bestselling author James Clear said, "Your mind is a powerful thing. The stories you tell yourself and the things you believe about yourself can either prevent change from happening or allow new skills to blossom."

Approaching problems from a position of being empowered and believing that there is a solution changes your mindset from one where you believe that your problems are bigger than you to one where you believe that you are bigger than your problems.

This shift jettisons you out of the victim, passive, woe-is-me role and into an active and strong stance. It opens up a myriad of possibilities that enable you to recognize the resources available to help you navigate your problem, as well as the perspective that problems can open up windows in your mind that may have been shut. This leads to creativity, innovation, and confidence.

Life is partly a series of problems, and believing that there are solutions activates the understanding that, just like each of the habits, solving problems requires structure and practice. None of these habits is passive. They all need you to do something, but it first starts with what you believe, which shapes what you do. Mahatma Gandhi said, "Your beliefs become your thoughts, your thoughts become your words, your words become your actions, your actions become your habits, your habits become your values, your values become your destiny." Carol Dweck's breakthrough book *Mindset* is all about how "What you believe affects what you achieve." If we believe that there is a solution, it puts us in the realm of positivity because we focus on what the problem will add to us as we work toward the solution.

Some might argue that a focus on solutions could be frustrating because there is not always a solution. But what are solutions? Many view solutions through a rigid lens or fixed mindset, where the focus is on finding an answer to the problem. Frequently, we know what we want the solution to be. **The Latin root "solu" of the word solution means "loosening" or "untying" of a complex problem, so the word solution is that which has "loosened" or "untied" the knot of the problem.** This introduces a fresh perspective of Habit of Positivity #1, where we believe that the problem we encounter is creating opportunities to "loosen" or to "understand, deconstruct, gain clarity." As you "untie" or "gain freedom and breakthrough" from the shackles of the problem, therein lies the "solution." When a solution is defined in that context, it releases you from the stringent and daunting task of always having to find an answer. Instead, you are engaged in a process in which you are enriched.

Habit of Positivity (HOP) #2

Convert a Limit into an Opportunity. In renowned psychologist Carol Dweck's research, she identified two mindsets: a "growth" mindset and a "fixed" mindset. A mindset is the lens through which you view the world, and it affects what you think, what you believe, how you act, and the choices you make. She defined people with growth mindsets as believing that their intelligence, talents, and basic abilities can be increased or enhanced through hard work and dedicated effort. She recognized the brain's innate plasticity and the ability for growth.

HOP #2 derives from the understanding that your problem should serve you, not you serve your problem. That means our built-in optimism, resilience, and perseverance come with a recognition that we can grow from our problems. Thus we engage with our challenges from a perspective of abundance rather than deficit, thus, extracting the opportunity in every situation.

When we approach our limits from this perspective, circumstances do not intimidate or deflate us. This does not deny that genuine feelings of disappointment, sadness, or frustration may occur. It is healthy to create space to feel, process, and create strategies for healing, but HOP #2 positions us to rise and not dwell in a place of defeat or hopelessness. When we stop to think about challenging situations and turn them upside down to extract the benefits we received from them, it reminds us that we turned lemons into lemonade before. We can walk with confidence and practice approaching challenges fearlessly because of the expectation that there is always a silver lining.

Habit of Positivity (HOP) #3

Keep the Positive; Discard the Negative. Dr. Rick Hanson, a psychologist, and bestselling author says that "letting go" is one of the five essential skills. We use letting go whenever we relax, practice stress relief, release painful feelings like worry or anger, take things less seriously, or drop thoughts that make us and others unhappy. Letting go requires an act of mindfulness that comprises being aware of the issues that need to be released allowing yourself to process the issues before actively releasing them. It is a process that involves giving yourself full permission to feel, wallow, and experience the emotions before releasing them. This conscious release is an act of power.

HOP #3 considers the mathematical functions of positive and negative. Negativity subtracts from you. The more you hold on to the toxic waste in your body, the more destructive it becomes. You will feel depleted, exhausted, and frankly, become quite ill. The same is true of negativity. The more you hold on to negativity, the more it will rob you of your mental, emotional and physical health. Negativity is also like room-darkening shades. As negativity blocks your windows, you lose the ability to see and truly experience the things in your environment that elevate you. Negativity prevents light from entering, leaving you in the darkness of hopelessness and despair. Eventually, your eyes can adjust in the darkness, but the world around you is shadowed, dull, and devoid of color.

Holding on to and filling up with positive emotions and experiences, and using those as your guide, create a sense of well-being that improves health and longevity. These practices are not only crucial for your mental and emotional health but also critical for physical health. Positive relationships result in happier people, which results in better physical health, less brain decline with age, longevity, and less physical pain. Positive people emit wholesome and appealing energy that attracts others, leading to positive relationships, which come full circle back to better health. Relationships thrive when parties can problem solve and not hold on to grudges or negative interactions. Thus, developing the discipline around holding on to the positives and releasing the negatives is a critically important habit in all spheres of life. Releasing the negative does not mean denying its existence or steamrolling over negative experiences without giving yourself time or space to acknowledge and process. It simply means that you must choose what you will allow to have dominion over your psyche.

Habit of Positivity (HOP) #4

You are unique with a divine purpose linked to caring for others. Martin Seligman, the father of Positive Psychology, has identified five factors that determine well-being: **P**ositive emotions, **E**ngagement, **R**elationships, **M**eaning, and **A**chievement. Finding one's purpose has been a topic of much conversation because, as Seligman identified, *meaning* is important to one's identity. In her book *The Big Picture,* Dr. Christine Whelan writes, "Identifying how your specific talents and values intersect with the needs of others is the first step to living a purposeful life." People who actively care for others have a more profound sense of connection and meaning and live longer. The knowledge and belief that we are connected to something bigger than ourselves and uniquely placed on this Earth for a purpose that no one else can fulfill, bring us into an understanding that we are not an accident, no matter what our circumstances are. That knowing confers confidence that anchors us and gives us clarity about our worth. Even when we are battered around by the tidal waves of life, it doesn't cause us to question our very existence.

Sometimes, trying to find your purpose can feel daunting. As I talk to young people, that question arises time and time again. As a doctor, called in my teenage years to medicine, I wrestled with fulfilling my purpose. Even though I believed that I was fulfilling my purpose of healing others, I still felt like I was called to more. How could that be? As I worked through my frustrations, I realized that I had assigned purpose to a single and static framework instead of focusing on my *why* in the present moment. When I shifted my thinking, purpose immediately transforms into a series of assignments rather than one deliverable. I also realized that healing extended beyond the exam room, and I could show up in so many ways and still fulfill my purpose. If you use your gifts and talents to make a difference in someone's life, then at the time when you have been positioned on that person's journey, you are fulfilling your purpose in that moment. It's that simple! When you think about meaning in this way, it fills you with acceptance, peace, and positivity as you traverse your purpose path.

Habit of Positivity (HOP) #5

Be Thankful and Believe! Gratitude and negative emotions cannot coexist. The simple practice of identifying and acknowledging the things you are thankful for establishes a center of well-being that changes the lens through which you view your circumstances. It catapults you into an arena of abundance rather than lack, and it positions you to recognize that even if all appears dark, there is still sun shining—raise the room-darkening shades! Gratitude helps to raise the shades to let the light in. A small amount of light is enough to see in the darkness. Sometimes the vision may not be immediately clear, but there is enough illumination for you to recognize that there is something there. The more gratitude you express, the more the light floods in, and the more clearly you can see the other side of your situation. This introduces the positive emotions of hope, joy, peace, faith, and courage.

Psychotherapist Amy Morin cites studies in her book, *13 Things Mentally Strong People Don't Do,* demonstrating that gratitude opens the door to more relationships and improves physical health, with grateful people reporting fewer aches and pains. Gratitude reduces toxic emotions, thus maintaining better psychological health; enhances empathy, self-esteem, and resilience; improves sleep; and reduces aggression. The practice of gratitude as a Habit of Positivity helps embed a mindset that flows right back into what we believe. This positions us for better emotional, mental, and physical health and improves our ability to cope and hope in times of challenge and crisis.

Everything begins with our mind. It is our most powerful weapon and asset and essentially establishes our reality. French mathematician and philosopher, René Descartes, formulated the first modern version of mind-body dualism and is generally regarded as the founder of modern philosophy. He coined the phrase "I think therefore I am", which speaks to the understanding of our thoughts shaping our very existence. Barbara Fredrickson, a leading scholar in social psychology, affective science and positive psychology, proposed a novel Broaden-and-Build Theory of positive emotions, which argued that positive emotions open the mind to creativity, curiosity and experimentation. This response results in opportunities to gain new intellectual, physical and social resources, which have been shown to protect well-being. What we think and believe influence our actions, which then manifest our reality. We choose what we think, and the feedback loop connects our actions to our reality, and then back to our thoughts, creating a cycle of self-fulfilling prophecy. This is why it is important to fill ourselves with positive affirmations, images and readings. Surround ourselves with positive people because their thoughts and ideas inevitably influence your thoughts, which then flow into your actions.

Parenting with the Habits of Positivity

As a parent, I have created Positivity Scaffolds for my child. My heart feels as if it will explode as I tell this story because my son Mark was born at barely 32 weeks after a long and painful infertility process and pregnancy. He weighed only three pounds and two ounces. Every day, I would marvel at the miracle of his consistent growth and development, but Fourth Grade felt like a year of warp speed growth!

Mark had written a poem about lemonade for his final English project and needed to create something that reflected the poem. Surprise, surprise, he made lemonade! He painstakingly decorated a big clear plastic dispenser with his colorful artwork taped to the outside. The day that the project was due was a picture-perfect Spring day, and our household stirred from slumber to frenzied in a matter of minutes. I was hurrying off to a 7:30 a.m. operating room start, and my husband, Charles, was scrambling to take Mark to school.

The lemonade dispenser radiated a kaleidoscope of color against the kitchen wall as the sunlight filtered through the liquid and psychedelic artwork. Check and double-check. Our bodies were hurrying toward the cars. My husband placed the dispenser on the garage floor to open the car door, and I heard CRASH, BANG, SPLASH, followed by a loud yell. *Lord have mercy!* The cover went flying, the dispenser upended, and precious golden, tangy liquid flowed down the driveway. My son's artwork was soaked, the colors blending, and the once full, proud dispenser lay on its side, a shadow of its former glory. I was on the way out the door and felt so badly that I could not stop to help with the disaster but heard Mark's squeaky voice ask his Dad, "Are you okay?"

My heart smiled. Mark's first concern was for his dad.

"We will make some more," Mark declared, "and it will be even better." And he did just that!

The project was a hit as his classmates were not so focused on wet, stained, faded artwork outside of the dispenser but the delicious lemonade inside. Mark had added vanilla extract, his "secret ingredient" that was not part of the original recipe, and this resulted in an epic beverage that classmates raved about for weeks. He had tackled the mishap with gusto and positivity.

Our son had automatically put his hand up to frustration and defeat and said, "Not today!" He applied the Habits of Positivity that had become a part of our lives. He instinctively knew there was a solution, so he did not become frustrated and upset (HOP #1). He converted the limit of spilling the lemonade into an opportunity to make an even better product (HOP #2). Instead of allowing the spill to push him into negativity, he focused on the positive that he still had time to make more lemonade (HOP #3). He was so caring that his first concern was for his dad rather than his project (HOP #4). He was thankful for all our help and believed that he would not be limited by the mishap (HOP #5).

Ultimately, it didn't matter what the outside of the project looked like; what was inside the dispenser was most powerful. Because we had been building Positivity Scaffolds around our home, Mark had applied the situation to a Positivity Scaffold. Instead of being discouraged, he "acted with the expectation of a solution." A perspective shift to believing that there is a solution no matter what the challenges leads to less frustration, less anxiety, and more feelings of being empowered. This is genuine resilience training.

Are you feeling a little hesitant about taking this journey? Are you scared about whether you can create your own Island of Positivity? Are you intimidated by negativity and wondering if you can stand up and be spunky? I completely understand. This is hard work, a daily grind, and sometimes it seems easier to capitulate to negativity. Don't be afraid. Negativity has put out a lot of propaganda on positivity and given it a bad rap. You have probably heard that positivity is a state of unrealistic idealism that you can't possibly achieve. Some have coined the term "toxic positivity," which means always wearing rose-colored glasses and living in a place of denial. They view positivity as a destination or endpoint. For me, positivity is a process that involves a set of choices and disciplines that empower you. A perspective shift occurs when you approach your circumstances *one habit at a time* by scaffolding your situation into a consistent framework that results in a positive structure at the end of the process. Even if the outcome is not what you expected, you will extract opportunities for learning and gratitude. If you apply this way of thinking, you will always arrive at the glass half full. This practice has far-reaching effects on your mental, emotional, and physical health.

Now that you know the 5 Habits of Positivity, we'll begin exploring each in-depth, starting with finding solutions to our challenging situations. Even though the habits are listed 1 to 5, there is no hierarchy of importance. In some ways, HOP #1 may feel like the most important habit because it positions you with a growth mindset that knows a solution is possible. However, all 5 Habits of Positivity have the underpinnings of a growth mindset and build resilience and grit. You will select and layer your experiences onto the HOP scaffold in the order in which they are appropriate for the situation. This process requires constant building, as each day is a new day filled with highs and lows. Let's go!

HABIT OF POSITIVITY #1

There Is Always a Solution;
Work to Find It!

CHAPTER 2

Unlimited Courage—
Inner S.U.P.E.R.hero

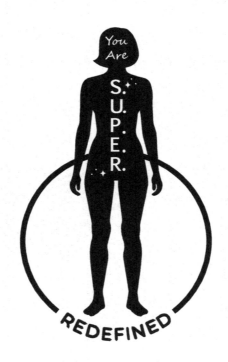

"I can do ALL things through Christ who strengthens me."

—PHILIPPIANS 4:13

"The new dawn blooms as we free it. For there is always light, if only we're brave enough to see it. If only we're brave enough to be it."
—AMANDA GORMAN

HOW MANY TIMES HAVE YOU felt that life requires you to be a superhero, dashing around like Superman or Wonder Woman, with all the invincibility and immortality of a superhuman entity? Are you taking care of everything and everyone around you so that the expectation of supernatural abilities becomes a measure of who you are? You have bought into the external definitions of "super," hook, line, and sinker. Because that is impossible to achieve, you move through life with feelings of inadequacy or not being enough. This has to stop!

*Imagine a place where we redefine "super" to harness the internal S.U.P.E.R. powers within—**S**elf-care, **U**nlimited Mindset, **P**ositivity Powers, **E**cosystem Living, and **R**ealisk Positioning (being real and taking risks)—that free you to walk fully in the power of YOU!* Not the unattainable Marvel-type superpowers, but internal "God in us" S.U.P.E.R. powers. A place where you see your authentic self and your unique powers reflected. A place where your S.U.P.E.R. powers defeat the insidious attacks of negativity that would cause you to run for cover in bed. Where is that place? It's your Island of Positivity on the inside, and you have unlimited access. It just takes courage to use your Habits of Positivity to gain access. Courage does not mean the absence of fear. It's pushing forward despite the fear.

How do you gain access? It starts with Habit of Positivity #1, which we will explore in this chapter—*that there is always a solution.* When you are in the midst of a challenging or traumatic time, believing that there is a solution can sometimes feel impossible. Remember that a solution starts with "untying" the problem, and you do have the courage to tackle that knot. Believe that you already have the courage on the inside, and that's where your inner S.U.P.E.R.hero can help. When you fully embrace this habit and operate from believing in your inner power to untie any problem, you will notice how much easier it is to get to a solution. So often, fear can impede believing that there is a solution, but when we understand that the solution is the process rather than a fixed answer, we galvanize our inner courage and kick fear to the curb!

Launching My S.U.P.E.R.powers after an S.O.S. from Dad

I have always felt as if I could do anything. Not in an "act stupid, tear up the place" kind of way, but more in a "there is nothing that can block my success as long as I had an education" kind of way. This was part of our culture. It may also have been because my mom left Guyana for the United States to complete her undergraduate education when my twin brother and I were eighteen months old. Though it had to have been tough for her, she did so because she believed in the value of education. If you have Caribbean roots, then you know what I'm talking about. Many times, parents left home to create better opportunities for their families. My father and other family members held down the fort, and we survived to be enriched by the wealth of knowledge with which she returned. Or it may have been that we went to an after-school class with Miss Imlah Ianthe Friday…a national Guyanese monument and treasure and an educator extraordinaire. She was like a one-woman army. Her expectations were so high, relentlessly pushing us beyond our limits, so that exceeding the limits became the norm rather than the exception. We were not patted on the back for doing what she knew we could do, and woe was the poor soul who tried to cruise, even if only for a moment!

I had fully bought into the world definition of "super": Be a trailblazer, excel in academics, attend the best schools, rise to the top professionally, cure all my patients, get married, have the perfect kids, look beautiful, never get sick, have dinner on the table for my husband every night, take care of my extended family, make money, and never need rest! Just give me my cape! I was going to be Superwoman. The traditional definition of what it means to be a successful woman is the invincible, mythical, otherworldly, immortal superhuman! If you are a doctor reading this, then you probably have had the same experience as I. If there is a friend or family member with a medical issue, I'm usually involved at some level. After all, superheroes are problem solvers, and even if the matter had nothing to do with my specialty, I was on the case! So, when

I received the call that my dad had a heart attack in Barbados, I sprang into action! This experience was a breakthrough to redefining my "super".

The day started like any other summer weekday. I sat with hubby in the early morning stillness, enjoying our easy conversation about anything and everything. I glanced over to the microwave clock and almost fell off my chair. *Oh, shoot!* How was it that time always flew by so much more quickly in the morning? It was operating Wednesday, and I was going to be cutting it close as usual. I did my hair, showered, and dressed in five minutes flat. I raced to the hospital, maybe over the speed limit, to check in my 7:30 a.m. patient. I arrived at 7:28 a.m. *Phew!*

"Good morning, Mrs. Clark; you ready?" I asked as I gently held her hands.

"I am now that you're here," she replied.

"Don't worry; we will take good care of you," I reassured her. With the final paperwork completed, I headed to the locker room to change into scrubs.

My phone rang. It was our Barbados home number.

"Hi, Dad," I answered. "How are you?"

His voice sounded less boisterous than usual, and he said, "I ate some soup that had been in the refrigerator for a long time, and I've been vomiting all night. I think it must be food poisoning. I don't have my car. Should I go to the doctor?"

"How are you feeling now?" I asked.

"Better," he responded.

"Okay. Just keep drinking fluids, and I'll check in with you later," I said.

In between surgeries, I called Shelley, my friend in Barbados, and asked her to check up on Dad. My last surgery was a radical prostatectomy on a patient with prostate cancer who bled profusely and took much longer than planned. My patient's wife was in the surgical waiting room, and as I entered, she greeted me with concern.

"You look exhausted," she said.

Usually, in my superwoman mentality, I would have denied that I was tired. One day, my best friend mentioned I looked tired, which I probably was, but I almost bit her head off because the mere suggestion that I wasn't immortal was offensive to me! It ripped at the core of what I believed to be true, but that night I was emotionally, mentally, and physically exhausted and had no pretense left in me.

"I am," I responded. "The surgery was tough, but he is doing well and in the ICU."

I left the hospital after 11:00 p.m. My brain was mush, and I could hardly string two words together. A quick check-in with my girlfriend informed me she had been in touch with Dad and would visit the following day. I collapsed into bed.

"Dad looks weak," Shelley said, as she visited him the following day. "I'll take him to the clinic."

I had never known my dad to be ill. He had some hypertension for which he refused to take medications because he insisted that his blood pressure was only elevated when he was visiting the United States. Being the doctor's daughter carried some weight, but not enough to dispel the fixed belief that one does not need to take medications if one does not feel sick.

I had another full day—crowded clinic, making sure our son Mark was settled, and back and forth with Shelley about Dad. Finally, around 8:00 p.m., as I grabbed a quick dinner with a girlfriend, and my phone rang with an unfamiliar Barbados number.

"This is Dr. Smith at Sandy Crest Clinic," the voice said. "Your dad has had a heart attack. I am transferring him to the main Queen Elizabeth Hospital."

It took a few seconds for the words to sink in. My entire body was trembling. My Dad had a heart attack? It just didn't compute. My head was spinning, my thoughts were spiraling, and if I had checked my blood pressure at that moment, it would have probably been off the charts. *How was I going to manage it all? Dad's alive,* I reassured myself. *Breathe and calm down.* I raced home. Thankfully, the restaurant where I was meeting my girlfriend was close to home. Before I called any of my family, I knew I needed to get my emotions under control and develop a plan. I had to believe that we would figure this out to get me past the anxiety and fear. I had to approach this systematically through HOP #1: There Is Always A Solution; Work to Find It!

First, I needed to untie the problem:

- Dad was sick in another country.
- I was the only one in our family who could navigate the situation.
- I had a post-op patient in the ICU.
- I had other responsibilities like childcare.

Then I assessed my options:

- How quickly could I get a flight to Barbados?
- Was there someone else who could care for my patient?
- Could someone else check in on Dad until I arrived?
- Who could help with clinic coverage?
- Who could help with childcare?
- Who else could help me think about the medical considerations?
- Who could provide spiritual and moral support?

Finally, I established a plan:

- My colleagues agreed to cover my patients.
- I rescheduled clinic patients.
- Friends and family rallied for childcare and prayer.
- The cardiac surgeon at my hospital agreed to offer whatever support I needed.
- One of my dear friends was doing a rotation at QEH in Barbados, and she could be my eyes and ears.
- I booked my flight for 36 hours after the initial call about the heart attack.

I love going home to Barbados for the welcome winter respite but had never worked at the hospital. My girlfriend warned me before I left Boston, "Oneeka, Queen Elizabeth Hospital is not Massachusetts General Hospital. Things move slowly. The ward is like Fort Knox, and visiting hours are limited. The doctors can be difficult to track down, so start breathing before you arrive and plan to be very patient."

I was exhausted from the rigor of the preceding two days of worrying, taking care of my patients, and preparing for travel. As I boarded the plane from Boston, I was praying nonstop for God to spare my dad's life. I was afraid that I would not get there in time. I didn't know what I would do when I arrived in Barbados. Still, I had to declare, "Not today," to fear and uncertainty and lean into courage, believing that I had everything I needed; otherwise, I would have been completely paralyzed.

"P" is for Positivity Power

I kept questioning whether there was any way for me to have identified what was going on earlier. Dad had experienced a massive heart attack, and his heart was functioning at only 15 percent. I don't even remember the plane ride to Barbados. Usually, when we approached Barbados, I would look through the plane windows and allow the beautiful sea-green water and the wide sandy beaches to welcome me home. On that day, my mind was in a tunnel, and the enchanting Bajan seascape fell on blind eyes.

I traveled with only a carry-on bag, so I disembarked quickly and went directly to the hospital. Many other families were waiting anxiously for visiting hours, carrying bags laden with food for their loved ones. The tantalizing smells reminded me I had not eaten for a day. I curbed my desire to wrestle them to the ground and ravage whatever was in their bags. I had fantasized that there was probably some stewed chicken, macaroni pie, and rice and peas!

When the doors to the hospital ward opened for visitors, the scene took my breath away. The ward was a large room with beds positioned in rows housing young and old men lying in various positions. Caribbean breezes danced playfully in the space, oblivious to the ward's infirm inhabitants. Sunlight filtered through the concrete brick wall's decorative openings, but I felt like I had stepped into a 1950s war movie. My stomach twisted in knots as I looked apprehensively for my father. I finally saw him on the bed, closest to the nurse's station. His breathing was labored, and the heart rate and oxygen saturation monitors displayed numbers that made my heart sink. Tears welled up as I stood next to his bed and took his hands in mine. His fingers were cold, his complexion ashen, and he looked as if he had shrunk to a fraction of his usual size against the stark white bed sheets. He opened his eyes, and I saw relief flood across his face.

"Thank God," he said, his voice muffled in the nasal mask covering his nose and mouth, "you're here."

I whispered, "I'm here. Don't worry and don't talk. I'm going to do everything I can to help you."

In the United States, my dad would have been in the intensive care unit fastened to countless monitors. He would have had one-on-one care with keen attention paid to his inputs and outputs, medication doses, and other bodily functions. In Barbados, there were limited resources to provide that level of care. Fluid accumulated on my Dad's lungs because his heart was so weak, and the picture looked bleak. My conversation with the cardiologist made the hair on the back of my neck stand up. They were essentially managing him with hope and a prayer.

My dad's heart was barely moving. His blood pressure was so low that he could not tolerate the medications needed to support his heart. All the cardiologists except for one and the cardiac surgeon were off the island at a conference. The heart catheterization lab only did cardiac catheterizations one day a week. There was no availability to evaluate his heart for another six days. When I spoke to the resident doctor caring for my dad, I heard a tone of resignation that they were doing the best they could with their available resources. He was likely going to die. Not today, defeat! Not today! I was not giving up on him!

Rather than crumple to the floor in frustration and hopelessness because of the staff's negative expectations, I reached again for HOP #1: There is always a solution; I have to find it. I realize now that I rallied my inner S.U.P.E.R. hero. I was like Esther in the Bible, appointed for a time such as this. I needed to launch the "P" in S.U.P.E.R.—my Positivity Power! I had to hold on to courage. Where was my Freeda the Flying Ambulance? Yes, that's what I needed! (Freeda is the ambulance that my girl super surgeon character, Dr. Dee Dee Dynamo, jets around the universe in as she solves problems.) I needed the real-life version to transfer my dad to my hospital in Boston, so I reached out to my Ecosystem (the E in my S.U.P.E.R.power) for advice. I called my best girlfriend, Paula, an emergency room doctor at the Lahey Clinic in Massachusetts, to determine how they usually manage international patient transport. Within 12 hours, I had contacted Air Ambulance to transport Dad from Barbados to Boston.

"U" is for Unlimited Mindset

Yes, I know that the components of S.U.P.E.R. are not in order! Stay with me! The resigned attitude of the doctors was exactly the limit I needed to spur me into action. Instead of waiting and hoping that things would change, I knew the buck stopped with me. We had little time, and I was overwhelmed by the magnitude of the decision. If Dad remained in Barbados, he would surely die. He could also die on the plane, but the best chance of survival was getting him to Boston. Everyone was counting on me. *Lord have mercy, it was a lot!* After lots of prayer, I had to make a choice. I believed in the internal power God had placed in me, based on his unlimited supply, and that was the wind beneath my wings. This was the assurance that I had everything that I needed. Unlimited mindset is the "U" in my S.U.P.E.R.powers!

I had 24 hours to prepare for travel. The Barbadian cardiologist needed to release my dad into my care, as I would be the responsible doctor on the Air Ambulance plane. This should have been simple, but the negativity monster was on the prowl. As the only cardiologist on the Island, Dr. Sewall was stretched thin and could not see my dad to sign him off until late that night. He was exhausted and irritable, and I felt like I had to be a superhero like Dr. Dee Dee Dynamo to save my dad's life. Dr. Sewall was frustrated. I was frustrated. "Not today, offense! Not today!" I had to put my hand up to negativity and call it out of myself to focus on the solution. I willed myself not to take anything personally. I had to get my father to the US, where the resources were available to better care for him. Not to be deterred, I remembered my friend's advice and the adage "You can attract more bees with honey," so I didn't get my undies tied up in a knot! I kept "killing" Dr. Sewall with positivity and kindness until my dad was in the ambulance on the way to the airport.

My dad is extremely generous and hilarious. Even though he could hardly breathe, he gave me a long list of instructions before traveling. The most amusing command was that I deliver some cassava dessert that he had made two days ago for Auntie So-and-so. Also, he suggested I pack frozen preserves he had made for his sister in New York so that I could transport them with us on the Air Ambulance. I didn't know whether to laugh or cry; Dad was the quintessential West-Indian parent! He was still trying to share what he had, even amid a massive heart attack!

I was already quite stressed, but I said, "Not today, overwhelm!" I realized that even though my dad's physical heart was malfunctioning, his emotional heart for others was intact, and I relented and whispered to myself, HOP #1: There is always a solution; I'll find it! This took me back to the trips home to Barbados during college. There were no limits to what

Dad might request! We would lug suitcases full of toys for Dad's community Christmas party and gifts for other family and friends. While on a spring break trip to Barbados with a group of resident doctor friends, they marveled at the fact that I was taking a large TV, lawnmower, and every food and household item imaginable as part of our luggage! Another West Indian tradition! Those were the good old days before 9/11 changed how we travel. To this day, any time my dad travels, he always takes something for someone. So, I asked my friend to drop off the dessert and reassured Dad we would somehow get the preserves to his sister.

48 hours after I arrived in Barbados, we were on the Air Ambulance Learjet to Boston. Chartering an Air Ambulance is neither inexpensive nor straightforward, and thankfully I could split the up-front cash cost with my mom (who lives in Boston). When I called to make the ambulance arrangements, they advised me it would take 48 hours to schedule a doctor to fly with the ambulance unless I was prepared to be the transport physician.

"Wait, what? I am an urologic surgeon, not a cardiologist!"

I had to reach down into my inner "God in You" unlimited mindset and positivity powers and believe that I had everything I needed and was trained to deliver whatever care was required. I now really appreciated those interminable days and nights covering patients in the Cardiac ICU during my surgical training. Even though I was afraid that Dad might die on the plane, I had to block fear, anxiety and panic, and stay in constant prayer. Thank God there would be a nurse and respiratory therapist on board, so I was not alone.

Be courageous and deploy your Habits of Positivity! You are a part of the solution, I told myself.

How many times do you pray for an answer to a problem, but it was not the solution you expected?

How do you respond? Do you complain and moan and groan that it's not the answer you wanted, or do you say thank you, roll up your sleeves, and make it work? This was undoubtedly the most stressful decision I have ever made and required every inner power I had, but I rolled up my sleeves. I called my mom and aunts and had the same conversation with each of them.

"I don't know if Dad will survive the trip, but I believe this is his best chance to make it," I said.

"We trust you to make the appropriate decision," they said.

Like so many married couples, my parents' relationship is complicated. In my family I am the event planner, travel agent, connector, caretaker, and doctor, and I'm always thinking ahead. When my mother moved to Boston, completed her master's degree, and got a job with benefits, I suggested adding dad to her US health insurance, even though he had coverage in Barbados. I wanted to be prepared should the need arise. For a host of reasons, logistical and otherwise, years went by before this was done. As much as I wanted to control the pace of the process, I had to "let go and let God." Often, we jump into the future to plan for some event instead of trusting and believing that we will find a solution whenever a problem arises. On July 9, 2008, when Dad had a massive heart attack in Barbados, and I called my mom to tell her, she said that Dad's insurance card—effective July 1, 2008—had just arrived. Hallelujah! Trust and believe that God's timing is perfect! Whenever I get anxious about whether I will find a solution to a problem, I just take a Positivity Pause and think back to times like this, and I am reminded that I don't need to solve the problem before it occurs. When it does, I know I will first untie the problem on the way to a solution, or the solution will declare itself if I stop trying to control the outcome.

"S" is for Self-Care

The Barbados skies were clear. I was so thankful because I detest turbulence. As I watched my dad being loaded onto the small, sleek Air Ambulance jet, I did not know what to expect. I was doing something that I had never done before, saving my father's life. I had truly stepped into my unlimited mindset. As I entered the tiny plane, waves of nausea assailed me. I swallowed the bile rising in my throat. This must be what it would feel like to be in a toy plane. Even at my five-foot-and-a-half-inch frame, I could not stand up. There were three to four small windows on each side of the plane. The interior was dark, and it was as if the walls were closing in on me. On my right were two single seats, one in front of the other, for the nurse and respiratory therapist. The seats had been removed on the opposite side, and the stretcher with dad was bolted to the wall. There was a flat shelf with a cushion and seatbelts in the back of the plane. That was my seat!

I felt as if my head was going to explode. As I folded myself onto the tiny bench seat, I had a lightning flash of insight. I had been up for days, had not eaten properly, and all this running around being superwoman would cost me my health. I would take care of myself with the same intensity as when I took care of others. The "S" in S.U.P.E.R. was going to be self-care, and that was going to be one of my powers—the power of caring for my temple and filling myself up, so I could then give from a place of abundance rather than deficit.

Without even thinking, I had assumed responsibility for my entire family. This is what we, as Black women and indeed, Caribbean immigrants do; we lift as we climb. So, when my younger brother needed to attend college, and there wasn't enough money for room and board, he lived with my husband and me. When my mom wanted to leave Barbados to pursue her master's, she came to live with us. When my husband's siblings and multiple friends needed a place to land during tough times, they crashed with us. As the first and only Black woman in the urology program, I was the only resident who had family members living with me during residency. I supported them, willingly shouldering their challenges, as well as my own. My stress level magnified in ways that I did not recognize; I now understand how these created silent chronic stresses that have played out in my physiology. As much as I felt blessed to be that resource for my family and friends, imagine how handicapped I was compared to my male co-residents, who cared primarily for themselves. But I survived and thrived, and there were so many joyous times and cherished memories created in our bustling household.

Even as I attribute making it through those tough times to my ability to extract the positives in any situation, I can reflect and understand that I had to redefine S.U.P.E.R. powers as first harnessing the power of self-care. I recognized the critical importance of recharging and restoring before resuming. As a Black woman in surgery, all eyes are on me. I have to jump higher and run faster to justify my existence, and do so carrying hundred-pound weights, while my co-residents have 10-pound hand weights in tow. My co-residents could put their weights down regularly, many times facilitated by financial support from parents, such as buying condos for residency, paying off student-loan debt, or funding vacations. While I have become adept at carrying those weights, and I have built strong muscles because of them, the long-term health effects are undeniable and the disadvantages stark.

How in the world was I going to survive this plane ride? Just breathe and have faith, I told myself. *You are courageous! You are a S.U.P.E.R.hero! Today, you are part of the solution to your dad's problem, but you are redefining some things, and you will be fine.*

Typically, I am a camel, trained by the long hours in the operating room, but I constantly needed to pee on that flight, which I did; several times. Into a paper bag! Don't even ask because I don't want to remember!

The flight was thankfully smooth. It was as if we were gliding in the air, and I had no sense of us moving. We stopped to refuel and cleared customs at an Air Force base in North Carolina, then landed at the Andrews Air Force Base in Massachusetts at about 2:00 a.m. Never have I been so happy to see a regular toilet. Dad slept for most of the plane ride, and I wondered how much of the trip he would recall. When we transferred to the ambulance at Andrews Air Force Base, the EMTs directed me to sit in the front seat. I was relieved because I had had my fill of tight, enclosed spaces. Immediately as I sat up front, I heard dad calling my name. He had sensed my absence, and it was almost like a child crying out for its parent. It was a humbling moment—a moment bursting with gratitude that he was still alive, that I was on solid ground, and that I had been chosen me to this ministry to be a part of the solution.

"I'm here, Dad," I reassured him quietly, and he drifted back to sleep.

"E" is for Ecosystem

After a forty-minute ambulance ride to the Intensive Care Unit in Boston, we were greeted by my husband Charles, my mom, and her close friends. The cardiac surgeon, who was a Harvard Medical School classmate with whom I had been communicating, had said, "Just get him to Boston, and we will take it from there." I handed off my dad with a sense of peace, knowing that I had done all that I could do up to that point. Sometimes that can be the hardest thing to do—to recognize when our part is done. Then I rested.

My whirlwind trip was made possible because of the support of friends both in Boston and Barbados, who prayed for my family and me and were on the ground in Barbados to greet me and drive me wherever I needed to go. They were the ones who fed me, provided a place for me to rest my head, and helped close up our home in Barbados to prepare for departure. My mom's friends and our Boston community helped to hold down the fort while I was away, and the medical community of staff and patients offered support and encouragement during this stressful time. The Ecosystem I lived in was the wind beneath my wings, and I identified it as one of my S.U.P.E.R.powers! "E" for Ecosystem Living! Even though it has been 13 years since my father's heart attack, the ICU nurses, cardiac PAs, and medical assistants on the floor still ask about my dad, who is alive and well.

As doctors, we are programmed to care for patients at all costs, so we lose our mortality and are perceived as superhuman. The night of my dad's heart attack, when I had to let the cape fall away from my shoulders and exposed my human side to my patient's wife, I was courageous, allowing her to see my vulnerability. She responded with compassion and concern for me, even though her husband's surgery had been more complicated than expected. That experience bound us together inextricably, and she and her husband had no resentment that I had to transfer his care to another surgeon so I could attend to my dad. They continue to ask about his welfare, even to this day. Both patient and wife needed future urologic surgery, which they entrusted me to perform, and thankfully there were no family emergencies or complications. Courage gave rise to compassion and connection.

"R" Is for "Realisk"

My dad was immediately admitted to the intensive care unit, underwent extensive testing and medical support, and had months of cardiac rehab. My dad was strong, and 13 years later, he is in better shape than many people, three-quarters his age. I learned from that experience that I had to stay true to who I was and not be afraid to take the risk of transporting my dad back to Boston, representing the "R" in my redefined S.U.P.E.R.power. This book is a manifestation of that "Realisk" power in me, a word I created that means "being real and taking risks." Being courageous and taking the *risk* of letting the *real* me be seen. **Vulnerability is a superpower**, and as per scripture, we are all fearfully and wonderfully made, so we don't have to hide. When you launch your inner "God in You" S.U.P.E.R.hero, whether it is a smile that changes someone's day or a flight to save your loved one's life, miracles happen.

S.O.S from Mom and God's Perfect Timing!

Are you beginning to see a bit of a theme!! In November 2016, I received the Youth Champion Award from EVKIDS, an amazing afterschool enrichment organization in Boston dedicated to serving inner-city youth. I wanted to see the program in action, but the afternoons on which the program was conducted conflicted with my operating days. Finally, I identified one day where there were no surgeries scheduled, and I made arrangements to visit. Lo and behold, the morning of my visit, I received the dreaded call that can fill a surgeon with anxiety. "Dr. Williams, where you? Your 7.30 case is waiting." Technology strikes again! I had upgraded my phone, and my schedule didn't cross over, so I was unaware that surgeries had been added for that day. For those of you who watch the TV medical dramas where the doctor scrambles out of bed, puts the scrubs on over their pajamas, and you think, that is so ridiculous! Why didn't they just take a minute to put on some clothes? I'm here to tell you that it happens! I literally threw my scrubs on over my pajamas and rushed out of the house.

By the time I arrived, the case that should have followed me was put ahead of me. I had to accept that as one of the consequences of being late…being pushed to the back of the line. As I walked up to my office, my cell phone rang with an unfamiliar number, and even though I don't usually answer my phone if I don't recognize the number, for some reason, that morning, I did. My heart stopped for a minute. My mom was crying hysterically, and I could not understand what she was saying. A hundred different scenarios flashed through my mind, each more catastrophic than the other, but I steadied my voice, reassured that she was at least on the phone. I kept asking, "Mom, what's wrong?" Suddenly, a male voice interrupted her sobs, introduced himself as the Transit Police and explained that mom was on the way to school and left her purse on the train when she got off at the station.

"Ummm, you mean she hasn't lost a limb or been kidnapped by aliens?" I asked with relief. However, she was so distraught, her life was in her purse, and she was now stranded at the train station. I reassured her that I knew there was a solution and I would come down to the station to meet her.

As I sped down to the station, I'm thanking God I had a glitch in my schedule. I thank Him that I was bumped to a later time. This was such divine intervention that I was approaching the problem from a place of gratitude. I'm praying that Mom calms down and does not work herself up to a heart attack, and I'm praying, declaring and believing that there are still good people in the world and someone will turn her purse in.

Superheroes are all around us with inner S.U.P.E.R. powers of kindness, love, compassion and honesty. Indeed, Officer Silen of the Transit Police gently stayed with Mom until I arrived. S.U.P.E.R.hero! As he was giving me the paperwork to file a report, my phone rang. One of my friends had received a call from a young man who found my Mom's purse on the train and called the first number on her phone! S.U.P.E.R.hero! Recognizing that I was a surgeon, Officer Silen offered to take my Mom downtown to pick up her purse and then take her back to school, a one-hour trip in total. I pulled into the hospital parking lot just as I was being paged to say the OR was ready for me to do my surgery!

Remember, I had to reschedule my visit to EVKIDS, which I did after the November 2016 US election. I have to admit I was feeling a bit hopeless on that day. When I got to EVKIDS, I felt loving energy rooted in service flowing through the room. The low hum of voices emanating from the pairs of college student tutors and mentees reviewing homework at multiple tables, blended into a calming melody. The chill in my mind began to dissipate. At the end of the evening, we got into a circle for the end-of-session ritual. We separated into pairs to share our joy and concern for the day and then shared what each other had said in the open circle. While half spoke of the election as a concern, the joy reports eclipsed those expressions, reminding me that the solution to hopelessness is courage and joy. The layer of icy cynicism that had encircled my heart shattered. Those young people had chosen to focus on the positives.

Later that month, at the EVKIDS Youth Champion Award banquet, I spoke about the power of personal narrative as a mechanism to empower ourselves and others and how that creates a framework to tap into our inner S.U.P.E.R.hero. I spoke of how the students owned their stories on a dismal day for many and instead chose to be courageous and extract joy. This was an incredible representation of who they were and an inspiration to me. They had launched their inner S.U.P.E.R.heroes, and I was filled with hope.

How can I not believe that all things work together for good? Suppose we are open to the notion that difficult events are the pathway to finding our inner S.U.P.E.R.heroes where we choose courage and joy even in the face of hardship. In that case, it changes our experience, elevates us above our circumstances and empowers us and others. Starting the day not knowing that I had a surgical case scheduled and the confusion that was generated could have stressed me out immensely. Instead, it created a jeweled trail of miracles.

UROLOGY STORY:
THE BLADDER KNOT

My daily interactions with patients are many times about "loosening the knot." Ms. Watts came to see me after having seen three other urologists. She had been dealing with issues of urinary incontinence and urinary retention for months. These problems were at two ends of the spectrum and required different approaches, which was incredibly frustrating. She felt as if she had been having no success at finding a solution to her problem, and she came to me with a catheter in place. While this seemed to offer a solution, the patient was in the emergency room every other night because the catheter kept pulling out. She lived alone, was wheelchair-bound, and did not have her own transportation. The trips to the emergency room were disruptive and frightening in the era of COVID-19. When I entered the room, she was angry, discouraged and unloaded all of her frustration onto me. No one was fixing her bladder, it was destroying her life, and she wanted me to find a solution to her problem.

I had reviewed Ms. Watt's bladder studies. Her bladder muscle was weak, so I knew I could not "fix" the problem in the way she wanted. However, I knew I could help her "untie" the problem and offer her a solution that would loosen the "knot," which was the burden of her urinary incontinence and inability to empty her bladder. However, I first needed to start by helping her "untie" her problem and understand the two opposing bladder issues. We could unpack and "untie" the fact that the medications that would help her bladder relax so that she did not leak would also cause her bladder to work less well so that she would be unable to empty. If I prescribed medication to make the muscles squeeze more effectively, thus stimulating bladder emptying, more leakage would result. Untying the problem helped lead her to the solution that I offered. I could surgically insert the catheter in a different location, eliminating her frequent trips to the emergency room while at the same time dealing with both her retention and incontinence. However, it would not restore her normal urination. Because I took the time to help Ms. Watts go through the process of "untying" the problem, she recognized the solution as the perfect one for her. She left the office feeling encouraged, hopeful and believing that this solution would work well. Imagine how much frustration and heartache Ms. Watts would have avoided if she had thought that there was a solution to her problem from the outset and she would eventually find it, which she did!

Inspired to Courage

One of my best sister-friends is Congolese, a trauma surgeon and critical care specialist. My husband and I were at the party where Ebondo first met her husband, Jay, one of Charles' best buds from Princeton University. Our friendship grew when she moved to Boston for medical school. Ebondo had moved to the US for college, and she told fascinating stories of that transition and her life. When we were together, I would listen spellbound as her lilting French accent transported me through rich and extraordinary escapades. I felt as if I knew every member of her family intimately before I ever met them. Ebondo's dad died in a plane crash in his mid-fifties, and Mamiere (her mom) became the head of the family. So, when "Mamiere" visited with my friend and Jay in December 2011, I knew I could expect many stories! The story transpired in a way that no one could have imagined with an eerie or divine string of coincidences.

Mamiere could not quite grasp the concept of the "man cave." Jay would retire to his man cave—a black hole in the basement of their home—for hours on end, and it never ceased to confound Mamiere! Unable to adjust, she defied all the man cave rules and would insist that Ebondo or their son check up on Jay regularly, under the guise of offering food, delivering the mail, or some other such trivial matter.

On February 12th, 2012, the check-up changed the rest of their lives. Jay's son found him in the cave, "down," unresponsive, and not breathing. Ebondo rushed to his side and gave all she had. Despite her heroic efforts, she could not do for him what she had done for countless others during her career—she could not save his life. Her 50-year-old husband was gone, leaving behind a twelve-year-old son, wife, mother, sister, and scores of family and friends who loved, admired, and respected him. A man who had featured prominently in so many lives as a friend, advisor, cheerleader, coach, and mentor was gone, and the hole felt like a gaping chasm. The shock and devastation reverberated near and far.

The loss was crushing. For weeks Ebondo would feel like an elephant was sitting on her chest, prompting multiple doctor's visits to rule out any heart issues, which had claimed her husband's life. It seemed almost impossible to wrap her head around what moving on would look like. One of the incredible parts of the story is that Mamiere had come to the US to celebrate her 70th birthday on a cruise with two of her friends who had both also lost their husbands in their early 50's. Jay died shortly after the threesome had returned from their cruise, and having dealt with a similar loss, they were able to usher Ebondo through this time in ways that only women who have walked in the same shoes could. With theirs and the support of family and friends, Ebondo picked herself up off the ground and cobbled pieces of life back together. She knew her son depended on her. I saw her launch her Inner S.U.P.E.R.hero to raise her son, care for her family and community while providing stellar care to her patients in ways that have left me amazed and inspired.

During the pandemic, Ebondo was on the ICU front line caring for COVID-19 patients. She was carrying a massive load taking care of dying patients; managing medical student education and resident training; covering trauma calls and other surgical demands. Ebondo was remotely managing the care of intubated family members sick with COVID-19 in Congo, where there are minimal critical care resources. Her son was studying from home and poised to graduate from his dad's alma mater, Princeton University, in 2021. Five family members, including Mamiere, now lived with her. Every time I spoke with Ebondo, I marveled how we would always find something to laugh about that would lift the mood even at the most challenging times. During one of our conversations, I asked her for one word that defined how she made it from Jay's death in 2012 to the end of 2020; she responded, "Courage." Somehow, for reasons that she could not understand, this was the hand that she was dealt, but she believed God would still work it out for good if she could only embrace the courage to fight on and not give up.

The loss of a spouse and father in the prime of his life is a tough, tough road, but as the saying goes, "when the going gets tough, the tough get going." All the traditional expectations of "super" now fell on Ebondo, as she juggled the family's emotional, financial, and physical needs. This comes at a cost, but redefining "super" is how we mitigate the price we must pay.

Ebondo and Jay had an ecosystem of support that they had built over the years, and it was indeed the launching of this S.U.P.E.R.power that helped sustain her. Their family and friends, especially the "uncles" who had become a part of the extended family, now helped father their son. As much as it is impossible to fill a father's shoes, these relationships helped to continue building on the solid foundation of fatherhood Jay had created. This, combined with the Herculean task Ebondo acquitted in mothering their son, has ushered him to adulthood as an honorable and hardworking young man, of whom Jay would have been so proud.

Jay had been treated for what was diagnosed as heartburn but instead turned out to be a symptom of heart disease. As the surviving parent, my friend now needed to take her self-care much more seriously. Like so many female physicians, we drive our bodies to the brink, juggling demands at work and home until our body screams STOP. She listened! Sometimes it required that she hit a brick wall. Even when she was flat on her back, she believed that there would be a solution to whatever was transpiring, and she approached the challenge with courage rather than hopelessness and self-pity. She took the time needed to recover and then got back in the saddle a bit wiser!

For her, focusing on self-care meant gardening, which allowed her a place for self-expression and relaxation as she planted and picked peppers, making a signature pepper sauce that is legendary. Like many of us, even though she knows that one key to staying healthy is regular exercise, going to the gym or getting on the treadmill just felt like another assigned task and fell off the list. She got creative and devised a family dance hour. This has grown into an annual dance challenge, where family members across the world learn the steps to a dance during the year and submit videos at Christmas, dressed in matching outfits for a dance-off. Infusing creativity, exercise, family time, and fun introduced a solution to several problems (HOP #1), turned a limit into opportunities (HOP #2), and is a powerful manifestation of why Ebondo's courage is a product of the Habits of Positivity that she has been practicing without knowing it! In actuality, Ebondo had developed her positivity framework, which she calls "PMA", Positive Mental Attitude. Her observation has been that "PMA" is a reliable predictor of patient outcome in the ICU, so she actively encourages patients to focus on an attitude of positivity during their medical or surgical encounters.

COVID-19 has been devastating and rough for everyone, especially frontline workers. For the doctors and medical providers delivering care with limited resources and placing themselves and their families at risk, it has been especially heartbreaking and an assault on their mental health. Yet, Ebondo never shied away from her commitment to care for others, approaching the work with courage and confidence. When the load became too much to bear, she spoke up, was honest, and drew the line. Articulating that she had reached her threshold required courage and strength. COVID-19 has taught her to delegate more, let go of some things, and find joy and passion in the "small stuff". Her Inner S.U.P.E.R.hero serves her well as she focuses on self-care and trusts in the unlimited inner resources that God has given her to step out boldly with courage. Ebondo uses her positivity habits to approach challenges from an empowered place, has the power of her ecosystem, which helps sustain her, and she keeps it real! She had taken her pain by the horns, mounted her saddle of courage, and continued her ride on purpose. This has been so remarkable and such an inspiration for me to witness.

Life includes a combination of small and large problems that we need to untie. In so many areas of our lives, we are called upon to develop solutions, which can seem overwhelming. How often, when faced with a problem, do you immediately interpret that problem as a negative? How often does the environment in which you are trying to address the problem feel negative? You may think that we live in a world where the default setting is negativity. Still, we can actively train ourselves to tap into our inner S.U.P.E.R.hero to approach our challenges from a place of power: the "God in Us" S.U.P.E.R.powers that allow us to launch Habits of Positivity at any challenge. These S.U.P.E.R.powers are not mystical. They come from an internal place of unlimited abundance to which all have access. It connects them to all aspects of our lives. When we think of ourselves in that capacity, we embrace our innate God-given powers, reject the external, unattainable definitions of "super" that deplete and diminish us, and reset to have an impactful and emotionally, mentally, and physically healthy life.

POSITIVITY PAUSE

I recognized that the runway to the problem was part of the solution in my dad's situation. I activated my "inner limit converter" and used the positives in the situation to provide jet fuel. I believed God had positioned me for such a time as this and allowed gratitude to be my turbo boost!

Where do you pull from when the external world throws problems and negativity at you? Have you been so indoctrinated with the external definition of "super" that you constantly feel like you are swimming upstream in a negativity river? How can you own your S.U.P.E.R. so that you don't feel as if you are functioning from a place of overwhelm and depletion? Habit of Positivity #1 is the first step. What do you believe? If you believe that *there is always a solution,* you approach your situation with positive expectations.

How many of you take a break and then feel guilty? That feeling still sometimes sneaks up on me! How many of you have a deep belief that the service that God calls you to is not meaningful unless you are sacrificing yourself to do it? How can you possibly sustain your output of giving if you are not filling up? If you continue on a path of giving without recharging, then you will ultimately burn out and crash, and then you are not good for anyone—your family, your children, your co-workers, or your patients. I needed to understand how stress could take a toll on me, even as I powered through; I had to redefine "super" to stay emotionally, mentally, and physically healthy. This is the S.U.P.E.R.hero you, too, need to launch.

You can do it! You can tap into your internal S.U.P.E.R. powers by practicing the following:

- **"S"**–Self-Care is the first S.U.P.E.R. Power. It helps you to redefine, recharge, and resume. Your Positivity Pauses enable you to create a discipline around taking time for **SELF-CARE: S**piritual connection, self-**E**xpression, practicing self-**L**ove, being **F**earless, **C**aring for your body, practicing **A**wareness, **Re**sting and **E**njoying.

- **"U"**– Unlimited Mindset.

- **"P"** – Positivity Habits.

- **"E"** – Ecosystem Living.

- **"R"** – Realisk Positioning.

POSITIVITY PRACTICE

Launch/Unleash Your Inner S.U.P.E.R.hero

1. Can you think of times when you felt as if you needed to be Superhuman?

2. Are you always able to live up to the expectations of the external world?

3. How do you feel when you do not?

4. Are you ready to redefine "super" so that you can give from a place of overflow rather than inadequacy?

5. Set the intention to launch your inner S.U.P.E.R. hero every day and spend 10 minutes at the end of every day writing how you have exercised your inner S.U.P.E.R. powers. Have you paused for self-care? Have you plugged into your unlimited by staying connected to your source? Have you practiced your Habits of Positivity? Have you spent some time in the community? Have you taken a risk to let your authentic self be seen?

TRANSFORMATION

Reflect on how you felt when you practiced not measuring yourself by external metrics, but instead focused on your internal S.U.P.E.R. resources. Journal your responses below:

Before I knew I had everything that I needed on the inside, I spent so much time trying to meet the world's definition of "super," and I used to feel:

Now that I think about my unlimited nature and how my power lives in me, caring for myself, living positively in the community, and not being afraid to be me, I launch my Inner S.U.P.E.R.hero daily, and I feel:

CHAPTER 3

Unlimited Hope—
Treasure Chest

**"For I know the plans I have for you,
declares the Lord, plans to prosper you
and not harm you, plans to give you HOPE
and a future."**

—JEREMIAH 29:11

"I'm flowing, I'm glowing, shining from the inside out!
Treasures stacked high from before I was born,
My gems are fearfully and wonderfully made,
uniquely me, never meant to fade.
I'm flowing, I'm glowing, shining from the inside out,
I am a Treasure Chest popping from the time I popped out!"

—DR. ONEEKA WILLIAMS

HAVE YOU EVER HAD TO fight limited thinking and negativity barehanded? Were there times when you were denied opportunities, promotions, or access to resources because of what you looked like or where you were from? I suspect that many of you likely reacted the way I did—frustrated, discouraged, and angry. Is there a way to train ourselves not to be wholly diminished or defeated by these experiences? How can you access a well of hope to find positivity, even in very grim situations? It simply starts with a choice and a declaration, "Not today, negativity! Not today!"

Hope is an important part of believing that we can always find a solution. It is like a lever that you pull to release the possibilities into the atmosphere.

You may wonder how you can learn to hope. I think of it as having a *Governing Positivity System (GPS)* that can be modeled and taught and begins with what we are exposed to in childhood. How do we foster that *GPS* within ourselves and our children. We do this by thinking of ourselves as Treasure Chests, overflowing with abundance and personal gems. We have to be intentional about uncovering the treasure and filtering out what doesn't belong. This process will always point us toward self-worth, positivity, and hope. In this chapter, I will share some of my journey to my *GPS* and hope, and I will encourage you to open your Treasure Chest and find your gems to help you in challenging times.

The Governing Positivity System (GPS)

I never imagined that hearing the words, "we don't offer physics for girls" 40 years ago would shape the trajectory of my life so that every day I open my eyes, I would seek to live the unlimited version of myself. I was initially disappointed and quite upset.

That was my first real encounter with limited thinking. But I used my voice, and that experience was the dawning of a new era where I would push past the limits of tradition, thoughts, self-doubt, fear, negative stereotypes, unconscious bias, and expectations. I look back and realize that I had put my hand in negativity's face and declared, "Not today, self-doubt! Not today, negative stereotypes! Not today, limiting thoughts!"

I didn't always know that I wanted to be a doctor. I talked so much that my family thought I would be a lawyer. My mother used to call me the "people's representative." If there was an underdog who needed to be defended or represented, yours truly was first in line! Frankly, it is an inherited trait. Our home in Guyana was a revolving door of family members, friends, students; anyone who was down and out or needed a place to rest their heads while transitioning from one life phase to another or just needed a helping hand in their studies or otherwise.

One of my most vivid memories occurred late one night while making the long and sometimes dangerous one-hour drive from Guyana's Timehri International Airport to Georgetown, the capital where we lived. We had dropped off a family member leaving the country, and I had settled comfortably into the red leather back seat of my dad's Morris Oxford, known by its license plate, PP500. I still remember every detail about the car. Dad kept the interior pristine. The cream exterior sparkled clean with daily washes and loving waxes, and the suspension was coddled so that the smooth movement lulled me into my customary nap as the car cruised down the desolate road. Better yet, the road was dark with sparse streetlamps, perfect conditions for slumber. Awakened by the abrupt cessation of car movement and loud voices, I opened my eyes to an accident scene that cars passing before us had ignored. Late-night criminal activity was prevalent in Guyana, and drivers may have feared it was a setup. However, my parents could not drive by, knowing that there may have been someone in need.

In the car was a family, one of whom was a young woman covered in blood. There were no 911 services, cell phones, or on-demand ambulances, so our only recourse was to squeeze her into our car and drive forty-five minutes to Georgetown Hospital. I remember the acrid smell of her blood, and I couldn't take my eyes off of her chest as if I were a built-in respiration monitor that would sound the alarm if her breathing stopped. We finally arrived at the hospital, and the second my dad opened the back door of the car, she leaned outside, and an eruption of molten vomit emanated from her mouth. She had been holding it in at grave peril to herself, lest she appeared unappreciative of the Good Samaritan deed of my parents. Caring for others was the scaffold upon which my parents layered their everyday life, and it was imprinted as our *Governing Positivity System* or *GPS*.

The *Governing Positivity System* has been passed down through generations. My mother's great-grandmother came to Guyana from India; she had two daughters, Aida and Louisa Ganjabir, whom everyone called "Ma". Ma was my mother's grandmother. Neither Aida nor Ma could read or write. Aida, however, was single-minded and ruthless in her goal to amass as much material wealth as possible, and she maneuvered her way into acquiring real estate and becoming a shrewd and uncompromising businesswoman. Ma's wealth was in her heart. Her small one-bedroom home became a shelter for anyone needing a place to rest their head or a meal to fill their belly. My mom remembers that even though they were extremely poor, she never felt that way because Ma was always giving and never seemed to run out. She provided solutions to the problems of so many others from a place of abundance. I come from a legacy of strong women with strong faith who exemplified HOP #1: There is always a solution!

This was the *GPS* that guided my grandmother, Doris, who had only an elementary education but provided support for her entire neighborhood with whatever she had. All of Ma's children had the *GPS*. My Granny knew the value of a good education, and even though hers was limited, she did everything she could to instill those values in her children, grandchildren, and anyone in her reach. When my mother was admitted to the hospital at ten-years-old, on the very day that she needed to sit for the high school scholarship exam, she could have thrown up her hands in defeat. That scholarship was the only avenue for her to attend Guyana's premier all-girls school, Bishop's High School, and there were no other test dates. Not to be deterred, my grandmother's and mother's *GPS* activated and they did not give up until they had found a solution! A proctor was sent to the hospital and my mom took the exam from her hospital bed! So it is not surprising that I have inherited the *GPS*. I am a "chip off the old blocks"!

The Call to Medicine and Activation of Hope

The moment I knew I wanted to be a doctor is seared into my memory. I was 13 years old. My dad was an outspoken critic of the Guyana government and as the political climate become more challenging, he accepted a job as the Chief Editor of the Caribbean News Agency (CANA) and our family moved from Guyana to Barbados. I enrolled at the Christ Church Foundation all-girls school. On most days, lunchtime could not come soon enough, the sound of the bell barely audible over the cacophony of intestinal activity! One day, as everyone dashed toward the door, lunchboxes in tow, I heard a bloodcurdling scream. It seemed as if time froze for a moment, with all eyes trained in the sound's direction. Blood was pouring (well, maybe it was just dripping) from one of my classmate's earlobes, her earring entangled in her uniform collar.

Without thinking, I moved swiftly toward her, even as my other classmates scrambled away. I could feel my heart pounding as I tended to her, not wanting to hurt her further. I disentangled the earring from her ripped earlobe, cleaned up the blood, and comforted her. As her eyes connected with mine in gratitude, it all felt so right. The lights flashed; the bells rang. My Super hero cape descended onto my shoulders, and I knew in that instant that I was going to be a doctor.

Unfortunately, it was not that simple. This all-girls school did not offer physics, a prerequisite for medicine. Folklore had it that some male teacher had tried his utmost to teach physics to the girls, and had failed miserably. He declared that "it was impossible to teach girls physics!" Have you ever had the feeling that you were being limited based on some historical experience that had nothing to do with you? How do you respond?

HOP #1: There is Always a Solution; Work To Find It!

Not to be dissuaded, discouraged, or to succumb to the status quo—after all, there was a super hero in the making—my parents kicked up a holy fuss and advocated for me. My teachers were on board, and I believed that there would be a solution because their voices were lifted on my behalf. My *GPS* and hope were activated!

At the beginning of the following academic year, my life changed. I marched into school as the only girl in the all-boys high school, where I would take physics and complete the rest of my high school education. I was 14 years old. With my freshly starched white shirt tucked into my gray knee-length polyester skirt, my yellow and blue tie smartly knotted around my neck, I was ready for my first day. Everything seemed surreal. I paused at the classroom door, looking into the curious eyes of my new classmates, all singularly trained on me, and suddenly my new reality hit me. I resisted the urge to bolt. "Not today, intimidation, not today!" I would not let them see me sweat. I squared my shoulders and walked to the only empty desk, up front and conveniently positioned next to my twin brother. His presence was comforting, even though I knew he would not babysit me!

Entering an all-boys school as the first girl was an unforgettable experience. I stood out like a sore thumb. There were days when I felt like sinking into the ground, and it was usually on the days when my menstrual cycle refused to play second fiddle to school. It descended like a beast, wiped out the competition, and a call to my dad would mobilize him to cart me home in the middle of the day, doubled over in pain. How EMBARRASSING! But there were also euphoric days when I went toe-to-toe with the boys, volleying and intellectually sparring as we discovered our shared values and explored the undulating terrain of our differences. Eventually, it seemed as if I had always been there!

While many might find this unimaginable, it prepared me for what would become an everyday reality: being the only Black female biophysics major in my Johns Hopkins University Class, the first Black female urologic surgery resident at the Lahey Clinic, the first and only Black female surgeon and urologic surgeon at the hospital where I practice, and the first surgeon to create and publish books based on a Black girl super surgeon superhero, whose adventures integrate Science, Technology, Engineering, and Math with Literacy and Habits of Positivity. (This creates a shared experience for all kids while modeling the power and worth of girls and children of color to encourage them to beat back limited thinking and win!)

I don't know how my parents scaled the enormous obstacle of their daughter entering a class of all boys when the pubescent hormones on both sides were in overdrive. There were no cellphones, e-mails, Snapchat or Instagram apps so my parents could monitor my social interactions with hawklike intensity. They guarded the lone home phone like the Gringotts dragon in *Harry Potter*. Despite that, I had a long list of admirers in the class. Nothing like being a jar of honey in a beehive! While it did wonders for my self-esteem and self-confidence, somehow, I knew that that did not define me.

I also found an unusual ally. For most of the boys in the class, Ms. Brownie, the English language teacher, was an old spinster who never smiled, was rigid and intolerant of any deviation from the straight and narrow. Her tongue could cut them to shreds without raising her voice, and they were very afraid of her. I initially believed that narrative, and I too was petrified until one day, she came to my rescue when my menstrual cramps were intense, and my parents could not pick me up from school. At first, I was very nervous in her presence, but Ms. Brownie became a reassuring and protective female presence for me. She lived in my neighborhood with her sister, and we discovered our mutual love of romance novels. She had such an extensive library of diverse literature that I spent many afternoons sifting through books and chatting on various topics with both her and her sister. It was with her I discovered my love of creating and working with my hands. I made my first pattern and sewed my first outfit with her — a knee-length jumper tied over both shoulders, gathered impishly at the waist, and made from colorful African-inspired fabric. When I put my hands in the side pockets, it conferred a swag that announced, "I'm all that and a bag of chips!" To this day, I am obsessed with jumpers of any type. The negativity of preconceived notions and biases was displaced by a delightful discovery—there is so much treasure below the surface.

I spent three years in that high school, and it became so clear to me that there is no way I could have survived if I had not been set up for success by those around me. I was a Treasure Chest that was filled to overflowing with messages of value and worth. This has sustained me through thick and thin and given me the hope and determination to stay the course. I always felt that my family and school staff believed I was smart and up to this trailblazing experience. They not only uncovered and exposed the value within me so I could see it for myself, but they also added to it. That chest contained my first Scaffold of Positivity, and it wasn't just my parents who helped build it. My teachers, pastor, family friends, neighbors, the clerk in the corner shop, along with the images I saw in the media all filled my chest. My admission to the Boy's school opened the doors for other girls to be admitted, and that knowledge filled my chest in a major way.

I look back at this experience in wonder and amazement. Just imagine if we transpose my experience to today's classrooms. What would it look like if we create an environment of positivity that embraces all the possibilities within our children? Even if tradition or stereotype declare that they don't belong; Even if they are the only one; Even if there is no precedent to support their presence. What would it look like if the goals of all educators are to set their students up for success no matter their gender, color or ethnicity? What if we roll up the status quo and make a play for real change? What if there is a uniting belief that "not even the sky is the limit" for students, and everyone in the educational system commits to being the fuel that blasts our kids into the stratosphere? I'm living proof that it can be done, and it starts with applying the 5 Habits of Positivity and filling up Treasure Chests!

Take Your Treasure Chest with You Wherever You Go!

I was bright-eyed, bushy-tailed, and ready to light the world on fire when I arrived at Johns Hopkins University in 1984. I had never been away from home alone, never been to Baltimore, never been in a dormitory, and never been on an American college campus. I had only seen the Johns Hopkins campus in photographs and certainly didn't understand the college drop-off rituals. My parents returned to Barbados before school started, so my New York godparents drove me up to Johns Hopkins, stayed for a few hours, kissed me, and waved goodbye.

I faced my empty dormitory room with two suitcases and my Treasure Chest. I looked out my third-floor Adams House dorm window at the flurry of activity below—students and families moving trunks, suitcases, and refrigerators into the dorms, the hustle and bustle of last-minute shopping supplies offloaded onto the quad—and suddenly, my lips quivered, the reality of being alone and on my own sprouted a fountain in my eyes. I did not even have a phone to call my family, but I had my Treasure Chest stuffed and bursting at the seams. I checked myself: "Not today, self-pity! Not today!"

I thought to myself, *close your eyes and take a deep breath. You are here to handle business. You have a dream and lots of goals to conquer on your way to that dream. Lives are counting on you. Get it together! You can do this!* I organized my side of the room with a few trinkets and pictures. I made up my bed with a frilly white lace comforter set that I had bought from a store on bustling Flatbush Avenue in Brooklyn, New York. As I viewed my whimsical nest, I felt momentarily comforted. Sometimes feelings of loneliness and isolation can be a slippery slope on which it can be difficult to stop the descent once begun. I put my hand up to negativity and instead grasped onto HOP #1: There is always a solution; Work to find It!

When my roommate, Mary, arrived, I attached myself to her and her family like a tattoo. I didn't let them out of my sight! Orientation helped me to understand the lay of the land. The biggest takeaway was to identify your resources and use them. So, I marched over to the Pre-Med Advisor's office to get my roadmap to success.

I felt as if I was an over-inflated balloon of hope, floating on the promise of resources to open doors to my medical career. In less than five minutes, the advisor had stuck a pin into my balloon, and I felt the downward tug of dejection as hope rushed out of my soul.

"You will not get into an American medical school," she said definitively. "Plan to return to the Caribbean for medical school."

When I asked her why, she said, "Foreign students are not usually admitted. You would have to be exceptional." It was as if she had dumped a whole pile of poop into my Treasure Chest. I didn't have words for what had happened to me, but somewhere deep inside, the words that bubbled up were "Not today, hopelessness, not today!" With tears streaming down my face, I dragged my Treasure Chest out of her office, opened it, and desperately started scooping out the poop she had dumped in. I felt like E.T., and the only thing I could do was call home! I stumbled to a pay phone, sentences choppy and sobs spilling from my core. Lordy, I don't know how my parents didn't have immediate heart attacks listening to me! They reminded me of what was already in my Treasure Chest. I was smart, a hard worker, persistent, and courageous. I belonged there, and I needed to activate HOP #1: There is always a solution; Work to find It!

What happens when you face an unexpected roadblock? You can find a way around the obstacle. Use your resources and ask questions. I had to find another advisor! I sought advice from other students who were ahead of me and at the medical school. We often have a myriad of informal advisors available to us who we don't recognize and access. I discovered a wealth of information and found an advisor who believed in me and was very encouraging. Dr. Cone invited me to participate in his research, opened his home to me, and became an advocate and mentor. I probably would never have established that relationship with him if the first advisor had not shown her biases. Three years later, as I was preparing to graduate a semester early as a biophysics major, I returned to see the first advisor. As I strolled into her office, Cheshire-cat smile from ear to ear, she looked at me dismissively. Sadly, she didn't even remember me. She had single-handedly created the first crisis of my college career, could have easily derailed my dreams, and yet I was not even a blip on her screen. She looked at me with barely concealed irritation, unclear why I was there. When I reminded her of our only encounter, informed her that I had been accepted to every medical school to which I had applied and told her I had decided to attend Harvard Medical School, her only response was not an apology but a disclaimer, "You are different."

How many times are destinies derailed because of negative unconscious messages passed on from generation to generation? During my childhood, I was fortunate enough to have conscious expectations set, which reflected a belief that I was capable. My Treasure Chest was full, and I knew what was in it. What would it be like if we set an intention to expose the gems in our Treasure Chests and those of our children and continued to fill them? What if we had a filter that allowed us to be mindful that whatever we put into someone else's Treasure Chest, or into our own, should adhere to the five positivity principles? What if we put our hands up and blocked any negativity from being placed in our chest, stating loud and clear, "Not today, negativity! Access denied!" Sometimes we even have to block ourselves! The first layer of that filter is HOP #1: There is always a solution; Work to find it!

Finding and naming my positivity powers has been like rummaging through a Treasure Chest and uncovering what is already there. I understand now that my early messages made me feel like I was full of precious gems. We all need this now more than ever. I used to power through like the traditional superwoman. I thought I needed to stand planted like a mighty oak tree, and as the winds raged and the waves pounded, I sheltered a soft inner core that never saw the light of day. It is difficult to bare one's soul, but the more I dug into my Treasure Chest, the more intimately I connected with my vulnerabilities. I realized they were an integral part of my positivity powers and not a sign of weakness. I had become so good at not allowing circumstances to keep me in a place of frustration and defeat that I had not stopped long enough to examine how the environmental and societal factors had weathered me to the point of physical illness. If I did not have this instinctual practice of positivity, I probably would not have survived. I observed this in one of my patients and how having her Treasure Chest filled made a difference in her emotional and mental health, despite a debilitating condition, and it truly inspired me.

UROLOGY STORY:
THE HOPE THAT FILLED SANDRA'S
TREASURE CHEST

Being on call for urology was sometimes feast or famine, crazy or benign. There were days when the beepers remained silent or nights when I was up every few hours with calls from the emergency room or inpatient floor. Sometimes a call left me incredulous, such as the day when a couple placed the husband's wedding ring at the base of his penis as part of their foreplay, introducing a stunning new interpretation of the vows "with this ring, I thee wed." His penis became erect, and the blood could not drain out of it because of the constricting wedding band at the base. He came into my emergency room, having to tell this embarrassing story. His pain was excruciating because organs don't do well when their blood supply is cut off. The solution was not simple, but there was a solution! We took him to the operating room immediately, restored his hope, and he learned a valuable but painful lesson.

Then there were some days when my heart broke, such as my call to see Sandra. I walked onto the neurology floor and reviewed her chart before I saw her. She was a young woman paralyzed because of an accident and unable to urinate. As I entered the room, her beauty took me aback. She had long black tresses layered in loose waves around her shoulders, smooth chocolate skin with long dark eyelashes that fanned across her cheeks as she lay sleeping, and rosebud lips that were formed in a tight grimace.

I said her name quietly, touching her right hand, "Sandra, Sandra." She slowly opened her beautiful brown eyes. "I'm Doctor Williams, the bladder doctor. I'm here to see if I can help you pee."

Her eyes filled with tears. "I hope you can," she said. "I can't walk, I can't use my hands, and I don't want to have this catheter."

The course since her accident was rocky, with lots of hospital admissions, uncooperative bladder with the problem of recurrent bladder infections. Her bladder never recovered, and I eventually performed surgery to reposition the catheter to her lower abdomen.

Sandra wanted to be a mother. She had lost a baby before her accident and wanted more than anything to have a child. Her family loved her and constantly filled her Treasure Chest, affirming that she was special just the way she was and did not need to have a child to be valuable. But Sandra believed God had made a promise to her about a child. She was so in touch with herself and would often speak of the baby girl that she lost. She did not hide from the grieving process and allowed herself to experience the loss fully. She was not resentful and continued to honor her child's brief life by engaging in rituals that kept her memory alive. She ministered to me without even knowing.

One summer, while vacationing with my family in Vermont, I noticed a group of laughing adults frolicking in the water and pulling an inflatable raft with a young lady they would periodically lift from the raft and immerse in the water. She would emerge looking like an ebony mermaid, sun, and water, creating glittering jewels in her hair. As they pulled the raft closer to the shore, a male lovingly lifted her off the raft to carry her out of the water, and I could not tear my eyes away from them. I marveled at his commitment to this disabled person, and it was such a feel-good moment. As the man walked onto the sand, I recognized him as Sandra's husband, Jim, carrying Sandra in his arms. Just wow! It was such a blessing for me to witness how this family loved and served Sandra. Her Treasure Chest was overflowing.

Sometimes we get as much from our patients as we give to them. My fertility journey began in the summer of 2002, while we were vacationing in London and Paris. I was exhausted during the entire trip, and I slept through our cruise up the Seine River, snored loudly during the bus tour to Champs-Elysees, Bastille, and the Latin Quarter. All I could think about during our Eiffel Tower and Louvre visits was when I was going to take a nap! When we returned to Boston, I had the most unpleasant nausea and took a pregnancy test, which to my surprise, was positive. Even though the pregnancy was well established, I developed the most excruciating pain that no one could explain. Four weeks later, at approximately 12 weeks gestation, I began to bleed, and we lost a girl. I took no time to process, much less grieve, and returned to work after two days off. The conclusion was that she had implanted on one of my fibroids, and I knew that I never wanted to feel that type of pain or go through that type of loss again, so we scheduled surgery to remove my fibroids before we would try again. That was the beginning of a dramatic journey where the pain and loss eclipsed our initial experience.

Listening to Sandra took me back to our losses, and I marveled at how her limitations had strengthened her. Whenever she encountered a problem, she remained positive, believing that there would be a solution, and she did not become discouraged. We had this in common. She often spoke of the hope and belief that God had placed in her, and it was palpable.

Filling someone's Treasure Chest can be unspoken and communicated simply by one's actions. Whenever Sandra came to see me, I was excited to see her and wanted an update of what had happened in her life the prior month, and my response to her filled her Treasure Chest so much. One day, Sandra came in overflowing with joy. After years of not being able to become pregnant, she had conceived and had an uneventful pregnancy. Sandra delivered a perfect Christmas gift, a fulfillment of prayer, prophecy and promise. Sandra spoke of never losing hope, as she now filled her son's Treasure Chest so that he always knows his worth and believes that there are no limits to what he can achieve.

Over the years, whenever Sandra came into the office discouraged about the physical challenges of keeping up with an active child to dealing with teenage shenanigans, we would fill up her Treasure Chest and reassure her she had made it this far, tackling problems as they arose. We believed she would continue to do so. She would leave much more lighthearted, hopeful, and reconnected to what she already knew to be true. There is nothing that God cannot do!

Do you know that there are many types of people who can help fill your Treasure Chests? Even if you don't have parents, your Treasure Chest can still be filled—it is not just a parental responsibility. In challenging times of crisis or personal loss, there is a tendency to assume a posture of lack, which exacerbates the emotional toll and physical wear and tear. Suppose we reach into our Treasure Chests to uncover all that is already there. In that case, we can filter through the crisis in a way that, despite the expected sadness, frustration, and disappointments, doesn't cause us to remain in that place of hopelessness.

As adults, we are better able to curate what is going into our Treasure Chest. We can actively fill our chest, but we still need to make sure other people are not dumping crap into it. External messages, especially those on social media, can also place feelings of inadequacy into our Treasure Chests. Being aware and having a consistent way to subject the contents of your chest to scrutiny can help guard against the limited thinking and negativity that would love to park themselves in your Treasure Chest permanently. The antidote to those poisons is the 5 Habits of Positivity.

POSITIVITY PAUSE

Do you know that each of us is born with a Treasure Chest, overflowing with hope and precious gems? They are filled with bravery, brilliance, courage, creativity, curiosity, kindness, generosity, gratitude, honesty, hope, humility, intelligence, love, persistence, and wisdom? As children, we depend on our parents and other adults to uncover that treasure and add to our Treasure Chest. Our words and actions are essential in helping our kids understand their worth. Others will often seek to dump garbage into our Treasure Chests, and we must be vigilant about not letting that happen. So, let's add a Habits of Positivity filter to your chest that prevents garbage from entering, and if it does, you have a process to remove the garbage so that it does not accumulate. Never give up on yourself. Open up your Treasure Chest and HOP into unlimited hope.

POSITIVITY PRACTICE

Fill Your Treasure Chest

1. Close your eyes and imagine what your Treasure Chest looks like.

2. Gather craft material and any type of container you have at home and make your Treasure Chest.

3. Reflect on who fills your Treasure Chest and write positive affirmations about yourself, remembering that these things are already in your chest—you just have to uncover and acknowledge them.

4. Look for the things in your chest that don't speak of your worth and remove them from your chest by writing them on a piece of paper and tearing it up.

5. Learn to apply your Positivity Filter so that at the end of every day, you can spend 10 minutes reviewing the events of the day and categorizing whether they should be added to or removed from your Treasure Chest. The HOP Filter must filter everything in the chest below.

   • Is it encouraging you to know that there is a solution?

- Is it empowering you to convert a limit into an opportunity?

- Is it storing the positive and not holding onto the negative?

- Is it reflecting your purpose of caring (for yourself and others)?

- Is it promoting gratitude?

TRANSFORMATION

Reflect on the difference between when you didn't know that you had a Treasure Chest and did not know how to care for it versus how you feel that you are consciously filling the chest. Use the Habits of Positivity filter to separate the things that belong versus those that do not and journal your responses below.

Before I started accessing my Treasure Chest and using my HOP filter to remove that which doesn't serve me, I used to feel:

Now that I fill and sort my Treasure Chest regularly, keeping all the things that speak of my worth and filtering out the negatives, I feel:

HABIT OF POSITIVITY #2

Convert a Limit into
an Opportunity!

CHAPTER 4

Unlimited Love— Life Fabric

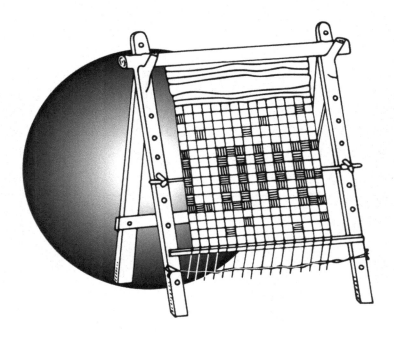

**"Love is patient, love is kind. It does not
envy, it does not boast, it is not proud.
It is not rude, it is not self-seeking, it is
not easily angered, it keeps no records of
wrongs."**

—1 CORINTHIANS 13:1

> *"Love is the essential existential fact. It is our ultimate reality and our purpose on earth. To be consciously aware of it, to experience love in ourselves and others, is the meaning of life."*
>
> **—MARIANNE WILLIAMSON**

HOW DID YOU GROW UP? Did you live with one parent, both parents, grandparents, extended family, or did you have some other set of circumstances? Is there generational dysfunction that weighs you down? What are your childhood stories? Did you have an unfortunate or traumatic event that disrupted your life? Have you had experiences where you struggle to reconcile interactions that seem hostile and destructive from someone who is supposed to love you? Is it possible to actively weave the fabric of your life to allow these dark life threads to be seen but not dominate your life negatively? When those dark threads threaten to overwhelm, hold up your hand and declare, "Not today, negativity! Not today!"

How do you build Scaffolds of Positivity and uncover your Powers of Positivity despite your experiences? Can you find unlimited love even in the most challenging circumstances? We all have a Life Fabric that tells a powerful story woven throughout generations. Don't be afraid to own your fabric. Show it to your kids. Weave and reweave your fabric using your Habits of Positivity, and you will help the young people in your life to weave theirs. HOP into unlimited love as you cope and hope in times of challenge.

The Power of Generational Threads

During the writing of this book, I embarked on a journey of self-discovery that was unexpected. I imagine some of you may have read the Treasure Chest chapter and felt that there is no way that you could relate to me. Maybe you thought to yourself, *her family is perfect, and mine is not.* She had parents, teachers, and a community invested and supportive, and that is neither my reality nor my child's. On the surface, you may be right. But below the surface, we are just as perfect in our imperfections as any other family! Writing this book helped me understand two things: First, parents or caretakers are children's first superheroes. They have a divine oath to protect, and I believe that somewhere in their hearts, parents want to fulfill that oath. My parents did their best to protect us and raise us the best way they knew how. Second, I came to understand that our life stories weave together in a fabric. When dark generational threads persist and become dominant, it is because we don't confront our stories and tell them to our children due to shame or embarrassment.

Our stories are so important. They are meant to be shared. They have power. They create understanding and context.

During the writing of this book, my dad shared stories I had never heard. These stories gave me a new insight into our family's strength and resilience and transported me to the place of unlimited love: my heart.

My Family's Unconscious Gender Roles Thread

One of the stories that my dad shared helped me gain a lot of clarity when my twin brother dropped a bombshell at the beginning of 2020. Maybe that should have prepared me for the crazy year that was to come! It was the first week of January, and I had resolved that 2020 would be focused on 20/20 Health for family, friends, and me. I was on a mission! I had always been the family health watchman, and for years I had been after my twin brother to switch to my primary care physician (PCP). She is knowledgeable, thorough, attentive, and accessible. The entire family had already done so, and he was the last man standing! My twin seemed to accept the plan until it was time to make the appointment. Then he asked whether there was a male provider as he would be more comfortable with a man. Have you ever had that moment with a family member where the unexpected happens, and it throws you for a loop? I was floored! As a female surgeon, I deal with bias at work all the time—I wasn't expecting to deal with it at home. The limited thinking villain was playing dirty!

My twin brother is one of my five heartbeats. My first Best Friend Forever (BFF). My first ride or die. The first person I ever cuddled with in my mom's uterine oasis. We touched each other first before we touched the world. We are inextricably bound. So, I pulled myself off the ledge and took a breath, and muttered, "Not today, family drama! Not today!" After all, I see many female patients who prefer to see a female doctor. That's not a bad thing. However, I needed to flesh out whether this was bias or preference. I put on my HOP #2 lens! I was going to turn the limit into an opportunity!

I asked my twin whether he would choose a lower-quality male PCP over an exemplary, better-quality female PCP, and to my surprise and dismay, he chose the male. Oh, my broken heart! I was so confused. This felt like a moment of crisis. Remember that I transferred to my brother's all-boys school as the first girl because the all-girls school I attended did not offer physics. So, my brother and I had been in the trenches, and I believed we were in sync related to gender equality. But rather than remain in a place of hurt, I put my hand up and yelled, "Not today, divisiveness! Not today!"

As I wrestled with making sense of my brother's response, I thought of my dad's recent story about his upbringing. My great-great-grandmother, Francess Elizabeth Osborne, was a dominant force in my father's early life. A shrewd businesswoman, she wielded her power unapologetically. She owned two large properties in Georgetown, Guyana, with 14 homes on them.

She collected rent, rationed water, and operated a bakery and convenience store on the properties. My grandmother, Audrey, and my grandfather, Walter, lived there after getting married, along with my dad and his siblings. My dad recounted that Ma Osborne ruled with an iron fist. She would "share licks" to his mother, Audrey, if she were displeased, even after she was married. If his dad tried to intervene, Ma Osborne would say, "You had better be quiet unless you want some of this, too." She would be clear about their options, "If you don't like my rules, leave." Sometimes they would leave out of sheer frustration and months later she would convince them to return. The move back was always welcomed by my dad and siblings, as they returned to mini rights in managing the property and having unfettered access to the many fruit trees, but the back and forth was disruptive. Certainly, their Life Fabric was woven with threads of Ma Osborne's love, their memories of her very fond and their entrepreneurial pursuits attributed to her early influence.

When my dad's great-grandmother died, the properties were sold off, monies divided, and everyone had to stand on their own two feet. My grandfather was bright and moving up the ladder at his job, but kept poor company with a group of drinking buddies, and went to prison for a time when my dad was in his early teens. As a result, my dad, his elder brother and sister, all then in High School, had to leave school and seek employment...one working as a wealthy neighbor's kitchen-aid, the second as an upholstery apprentice, and my dad as a cabinetmaker's apprentice...their earnings going to support the family. My dad recalls every Friday afternoon giving his pay envelope to his mom and she returning a small portion to him as an "allowance".

For some of you reading this book, this may sound familiar. As a youngster, you may have assumed a parental role in your household for various reasons. Maybe you were in a single-parent home, and your parent was working multiple jobs. Hence, as the oldest, you became responsible for caring for your siblings and performing other household duties. Or some economic hardship or unfortunate health event within your family forced you to step up. If you lived in the Caribbean, perhaps your parents migrated to the US, Canada, or the UK in search of better opportunities and left you with relatives until they could "send" for you and your siblings. Or you were sent to live with relatives for better educational opportunities and had to assume the responsibilities of parenting yourself.

My dad's older brother died when my dad was in his late teens, and his father, having never quite recovered, plagued with illness and job loss, died a few years later. As the remaining male, my dad assumed the protective role as the "man" of the house and my grandmother and aunts treated him with reverence. My grandmother could have crumbled under the unimaginable and crushing grief of losing both her husband and son. Instead, she rose up resilient, full of faith and strength, to care for and lead her family. She earned income by doing laundry and selling baked goods. So legendary were her cakes and pastries that her specialty "black" cakes were in the demand across the world as Christmas and wedding cakes. I can boast of the six layer cake that she made for my wedding when she was 80 years old! She became the beloved matriarch of our family and was the glue that held us together. When Audrey Agatha Williams, fondly known as "Motherdry", died at 102 years old, she left a rich legacy of love, generosity, service, community, determination and grit that lives on in us.

I recently learned of the term "Parentification," which brought even more clarity to my dad's experience. It was just happenstance that the term came to my attention. In February 2020, as part of William James College's (WJC) Black History Month Celebrations, Dr. Natalie Cort, the director of WGC's Black Mental Health Graduate Academy, invited me to speak. I presented on "Habits of Positivity: Transform Your Thinking & Change Your World." One of the young women there, Dr. Michelle Codner, later asked me to be the facilitator for her clinical psychology doctoral thesis because she knew I was from the Caribbean and focused on a holistic approach to educating and empowering children and adults. Her thesis was about parentification in Jamaican American adults and how this impacted excessive caregiving in romantic relationships. And I said, "Could you repeat that, please?" But it brought a new understanding of how children are catapulted into caretaking adult roles and how that affects them later in life. It gave me a new lens through which to view my dad's Life Fabric, my brother's, and my own.

I pondered how the thread of gender roles became so prominent in my dad's life and how this could have been passed down to my brother. Besides these beliefs being a significant part of our Caribbean culture, I wondered if, on some level, my dad might have attributed his great-grandmother's dominance as a factor in his family's difficulties and his father's need to escape on the weekend. Did this experience create a dark hue in his Life Fabric? Even as my dad encouraged me to shoot for the stars, there was a profoundly ingrained thread of well-defined roles with the male as the head of household, associated with specific actions and responsibilities. In my dad's case, that thread grew out of necessity, but it is also a thread that features prominently in many cultures. If we are not vigilant, these threads accumulate, are buried in our unconscious, and take prominence as a dark hue in our fabric. This affects how we respond to specific situations, the things we say, the decisions we make, and how we interact with the people around us, consequently communicating a set of biases. So, I interpreted that my brother's response was based on a gender bias that male doctors were superior to female doctors.

The Fabric of Unlimited Love

After I wrote of my experience and perception, I gave the chapter to my brother to read, curious about how it would resonate with him. It was transformational for him. We often have a bias that we are not aware of until it is brought to our attention. He stepped back to ask himself why he felt more comfortable with a male doctor than a female. He identified that he associated intimacy with being undressed in the presence of someone of the opposite sex, especially when his body was the center of discussion. There is a dissonance of context that could be a platonic or business interaction related to the body with someone of the opposite sex. This is also a deeply rooted belief in cultural norms, but it differed from my assigned reason. This awareness offered an awakening for my brother and more understanding of how we often jump to conclusions as we apply our perception as truth. This experience might have generated issues that festered for years but instead provided an opportunity for growth and clarity. We used this as an opening to explore how we felt.

How do you put your hand up, declare "Not today," block negativity, and HOP into unlimited love in situations when those closest to you disappoint you? It is always tempting to generalize that one incident as your entire relationship. First, the limit you encounter allows you to step back and gain perspective, which is an opportunity to acknowledge the good things in your relationship. The second benefit of consciously activating HOP #2—Convert a limit into an opportunity— enables you to gain more clarity and understanding.

Start in your heart with the unlimited love that lives there. Love is the glue that holds the Positivity Scaffold together. As I viewed my dad's Life Fabric from a place of love, it opened my understanding of why these threads had a dominant place in his fabric, and I had so much empathy. My dad's tenacity and resilience inspired me. Despite being pulled out of school, he continued to read whatever he could get his hands on. His younger sister became a house cleaner for the owner of Guyana's main newspaper, and she asked whether he might offer my dad a job, as my dad was very bright and did not like being a cabinet maker. Dad started as a copyholder in the newsroom. However, he was so diligent that he was promoted to a proofreader, and the subeditors had assigned him one of their tasks…creating the article headlines. When the chief editor realized that dad was the one generating the headlines, he was promoted to subeditor. They invested in him, paid for him to go to journalism school, and he rose through the ranks to become one of the most prolific journalists in the Caribbean. Similarly, because of these early experiences, my aunts developed a work ethic that secured their later success. One of my aunts rose to a supervisory position at the London Transport. Another became a senior officer at the American Insurance Group headquarters in New York. The third became a phenomenal leather designer, working with high-end clothing brands in New York. They converted their early limits into opportunities.

By focusing on love, and extending the benefit of the doubt, my brother and I could convert a challenging interaction into an opportunity that allowed us to spin lighter threads of understanding into our fabric and pass those down from generation to generation.

The Habits of Positivity create the loom upon which our Life Fabric is spun.

The loom frames and shapes the fabric, but we select the threads and choose how they are positioned within the fabric. We can think of our fabric as having multiple layers, and the Habits of Positivity allow us to position the light and dark threads from a perspective where we ask ourselves the following questions:

- Did the situation allow you to find solutions?

- Did you experience limits so that you can now reflect on the opportunities?

- Did you take time to process and make space to wrestle with the negatives but then rise from under them and hold on to the positives?

- Can you look back and, despite the circumstances, know and believe that you are uniquely created and full of worth?

- Despite the circumstances, can you identify things for which you are thankful?

There are so many threads in our families that create rich and textured fabrics. We have to choose to weave the threads from a perspective of positivity. I could look at my dad's fabric and see how his early experiences added threads of strength and resilience to his character. Those were elements that contributed to my success because he wanted a better life for his children. I saw how he used HOP #2 to turn the limits of his situation into an opportunity. I could also look at all the positive attributes in my dad reflected in my brother.

There is a part in each parent's heart with unlimited, unconditional love for their child. Even if that love is buried deep in their fabric and challenging to access, it is still there. This journey has taught me that we each have a Life Fabric to weave and reweave. Our Positivity Loom, which is held together by love, allows us to do so without shame, blame, judgement or regret. If we can frame situations in our lives from the perspective of how experiences have added to us, we learn to quickly pivot to HOP #2: Convert a limit into an opportunity.

I appreciated my parents' fabric for all its imperfections. I could learn its patterns and hues and feel its strength and textures. I could love them in all their nuances, complexities and idiosyncrasies. It's so important not to hide from the dark threads in our fabric. It is consciousness and awareness of all threads that lead to healing, growth, and stemming the propagation of negative generational patterns.

UROLOGY STORY: HOW MISS JONES WOVE HER PAIN INTO PURPOSE ON HER POSITIVITY LOOM

By embracing your stories as an integral part of your life's journey, you will gain an appreciation for the power of those stories as sources of encouragement, empowerment, and understanding. Please share your stories and weave them onto your Habits of Positivity Loom. Share your hardships and struggles, as well as your joyful experiences and victories. Please share them with your children and the young people in your life. Teach them how to weave their fabrics onto their looms. Do not remain bound to shame and pride. Let your Life Fabric, with its hues and textures of lived experiences, be seen.

I selected the thread from the encounter with my twin brother and positioned it on the Positivity Loom in a way that fought back against negativity. Whereas the villain was seeking to steal and limit my love, it introduced HOP #2—an opportunity to understand my dad and brother better.

I could have become so stuck in the hurt of my brother's response. Instead, I said "Not today" to negativity and used the Habits of Positivity to build bridges of understanding and love and transform my thinking.

POSITIVITY PAUSE

The threads in your life are the stories accumulating every day being spun into your bolts of fabric. Some threads are bold, thick fibers that can take on huge prominence; others are fine threads that weave together almost unnoticed. Thick threads can have rich colors, vibrant and stimulating—those incredibly happy moments that uplift you for the rest of your life. Sometimes thick fibers can have dark, despondent, and dull colors, representing traumatic experiences, which leave an indelible mark on your psyche and pull you into the depths of despair and negativity.

Throughout the seasons of your life, the fabric that you weave may be different. Sometimes it is woven as a tapestry meant to be viewed by many for its beauty. It may be woven like fine silk that is soft and luxurious and builds and triggers emotions that can be joyful, healing, or nostalgic. The fabric may also be a rugged canvas, durable and monochromatic, designed for survival. Whatever the type of fabric, it is unapologetically yours created from your experiences.

You understand that the fabric's richness and texture—the same hues and patterns—create interest, intrigue, and strength. The interplay of all threads results from the variability of life and gives meaning and context to your life. What does that mean for you? Can you choose how you weave the threads? Yes, you can! You can choose how you position the threads using your Habits of Positivity Loom. You can choose the patterns. It requires pausing, seeing the threads (consciousness), and then actively weaving or reweaving with love.

POSITIVITY PRACTICE
Weave Your Life Fabric

1. Meditate on what your Life Fabric looks like and find those threads of self-love and love for others.

2. Reflect on experiences that have created bright and cheery threads.

3. Reflect on experiences that have created dark, rough threads.

4. Think about how you might position the threads to create patterns so that the dark threads don't overwhelm your fabric.

5. Keep a Fabric Board where you think about the day's experiences, apply the Habit of Positivity Loom, and then position the day's threads. Even if there are days when there may be more dark threads, you can still apply the HOP Loom to help gain perspective and an opportunity to love.

TRANSFORMATION

Reflect on when you were unaware of weaving your story versus how you feel about the Loom of Positivity of your Life Fabric. You are positioning the threads of your life stories on your HOP Loom with love, and journal your responses below:

Before I started weaving my Life Fabric on my Habits of Positivity Loom and finding the purpose in my stories, I used to feel:

Now that I weave my fabric daily on my Habits of Positivity Loom, I see the dark threads, but they do not overwhelm my Life Fabric, and I feel:

CHAPTER 5

Unlimited Joy—Joy Tank

"I have told you this so that my JOY may be in you and that your JOY may be complete."

—JOHN 15:11

"Joy is a gift from heaven
A flame burning bright
That never goes out
Even if a fierce wind blows with all its might."

—DR. ONEEKA WILLIAMS

HAVE YOU EVER HAD SOMETHING so devastating happen to you it took your breath away? Where the pain was so intense that you eventually stopped feeling and went numb as a protective reflex? Something you could not even process or comprehend so that your brain, feeling as if it would explode trying to figure things out, tripped the safety release valve and shut down? How do you shift from a place of such intense pain to a place of joy? Not happiness, which depends on external circumstances to generate a feel-good emotion that makes you feel all warm and fuzzy inside, but absolute joy. Joy is the inner sense of well-being that is selfless and connects you to something bigger than yourself.

There is joy in a tank that is deep inside and consists of a knowing that we are not alone in the darkness. There is a light that we can't see because we have closed our eyes, minds, and hearts to block out the pain. If we open our eyes and hearts to the possibility that we will make it through, we begin to unkink the hoses attached to our Joy Tank and set an intention to turn them on one Habit of Positivity at a time. Calling upon our Joy Tank can help us convert what appear to be limits into potential opportunities as we uncover the purpose in every situation.

Finding Joy in an Unknown Purpose

The high-risk obstetrician office began to feel alarmingly like home. Blue subdued wallpaper and a smattering of floral prints on the wall greeted me as I entered the office. I was six months pregnant with twin boys, Matthew and Mark, and this office had become a lifeline, so I was not complaining. It had been a long haul to get to this point, and I had finally lowered my guard after the battery of genetic tests, high-level ultrasounds, cervical cerclage (a cervical stitch to keep cervix closed in hope of preventing premature delivery), and bed rest. I thought I could now breathe easier. Even the weather was aligned with this hopeful shift. May ushered in sun-filled mornings that sparkled hello as I opened my eyes and listened to the joyful chirps of birds preparing for their season of procreation.

That I was forty pounds heavier, constantly in pain, and struggling to keep up my clinical responsibilities in a practice of highly insensitive and unevolved men was a small price to pay for the gift of the two lives growing in me. Everyone in the family was excited and cautiously optimistic. They had been waiting for this moment for well over a decade. We had got the "when are you having kids" question from the day that we got married, and now fourteen years later, we could finally answer, "NOW!"

My husband, Charles, and I prepared for the routine previsit ultrasound in the small dark room, chatting casually with each other. As the technician checked up on our twin boys, we were so excited. My friends had finally sent out baby shower invitations with a "Two Peas in the Pod" theme with the two cutest little Brown baby faces peeking out from the pod.

I asked the ultrasound tech, "How are things?"

"The doctor will be right in," she replied, leaving. This was not unusual, as many ultrasound technicians are busy running between rooms and do not share clinical findings.

Doctor Hall entered, his typical bearded smile absent, and said in a soft but clipped British accent, "I'm so sorry, but I have some bad news. One baby does not have a heartbeat. Baby A has died." It was so abrupt and devastatingly unexpected, but I guess there was no other way for him to tell us.

I could not breathe. Searing pain ripped through my chest, and Niagara Falls tumbled down my face. We had lost our Matthew for no discernible reason, and it was incomprehensible. I could not think. I could not speak. I could not say the words. As if saying it out loud would completely obliterate the kernel of hope that maybe this was just a bad dream that I would wake up from. Charles had the arduous task of calling our close friends and family. Their sadness would only send me into a tailspin of my grief, so I hid under the covers. We had such an outpouring of love and support—food and prayers and words of encouragement—but I still felt as if I were suffocating.

How was I going to face the next fourteen weeks? Our son had been a fully formed baby. We watched the boys grow with every ultrasound, and we kept track of the increase in their weight and height with such optimism. Now one of my sons was dead, and I would have to carry him—along with our other son who was still alive—and live with the heart-stopping fear of a similar outcome for Mark. Everything in my life was put on hold at that moment, and frankly, nothing else mattered. My doctor placed me on immediate bed rest, which was just as well because I didn't see how I would drag myself out of bed. But for Mark, I needed to infuse all the positive energy possible. Looking back, I realized that even in the flood of tears, I had set an intention to switch over to HOP #2: Convert a limit into an opportunity.

"Not today, fear! Not today!" I had to focus on the opportunity to be more mindful in the present, the gift of the moment, and to give thanks for each moment of Mark's life and Matthew's life. It was so tough not to jump ahead to all the "What ifs." Every time my brain would pivot, I had to focus on not becoming fear's puppet. I had to focus on what I had instead of what I didn't have. I thanked God for Matthew's brief life. I had to work on what I believed and strengthen my faith and trust God that all things would work together for good. There were days when I lay in bed feeling broken, sad and disappointed, and I permitted myself to grieve, but then I had to turn my back to despair and declare that it would not prevail. "Not today, despair! Not today!" I had been placed on "bed rest" after Matthew's death so I physically had no place to run. The battle was all in my mind.

I focused on visualizing Mark as healthy and sending those thoughts inward. I thanked God for Mark's miraculous life, trusting, believing, declaring, and giving thanks; he was going to be born to live out his purpose of touching those around him.

A few days after we lost Matthew, Charles went to the plant nursery. We agreed we would plant a tree in his memory—one that would bloom every year on his anniversary. We selected a magnolia. Magnolias are thought to be one of the first flowering plants on Earth, and their composition has not changed. Just like God's love for us. The white magnolia symbolizes beauty, eternity, nobility, and perseverance in our yard and blooms white flowers on Matthew's anniversary to remind us of the precious gift that he was.

It was a tough time, and I had lots of heartbreaking moments when I would see Matthew laying guard over the entrance to my cervix with every ultrasound. Every time I saw him, my mind would sprint away from me to what could have been, and I would have to yank myself back to the present and quickly fumble for the nozzles of my Joy Tank hoses and turn them on my situation. As a style and fashion lover, I had bought a ton of cute maternity clothes and had nowhere to wear them except for my doctor's visits. So, I carved out the time and mental space to still do the things that brought me joy, and I got dressed up for every doctor's visit. I never wore the same outfit twice, and similar to my patients who often wait with bated breath to see what I am wearing on any day, so too did the OB office staff look forward to my outfit of the day. Those small squeezes of the Joy Tank nozzles release the joy within you and spread it around, even in the toughest of times.

Then miracles began to occur right in front of us. My cervix shortened, and I started having premature contractions. It seemed as if the only thing keeping Mark in my uterus was Matthew, positioned over my cervix. Mark had his angel and protector—Matthew was fulfilling the purpose for which he had been created. My gratitude hose connected to my Joy Tank was on full blast. I was so grateful. Now, whenever I saw Matthew holding position, even though the deluge of sadness was always present, the sight of him also overwhelmed me with joy and gratitude. I was so thankful that Mark was alive and still in my uterus.

When you extract the good from challenging experiences, a shift occurs. HOP #2—Converting a limit into an opportunity—offers acceptance that you may not have thought possible.

Experiencing Grief and Gratitude Simultaneously

My best friend, Paula, had convened a group of friends to plan my baby shower. They had everything ready to celebrate two babies, and she was devastated by the loss because she knew the pain and struggle involved in getting to this point. How could they pull off a shower while I was on bedrest? Paula wanted to celebrate the blessing that we still had a living child, but she didn't know if the whole occasion would be too painful for me. She persisted, focusing on the joy that was a part of the blessing we could still celebrate. She pivoted from fear and disappointment to positivity and celebration. She embraced the Habits of Positivity and turned the limit into an opportunity to be inventive and resourceful.

The morning of the shower dawned bright, sunny, and clear, and I could hear the flurry of activity from my basement bedroom. I had relocated there to avoid climbing stairs as I went back and forth to my doctor's appointments. As I lay sequestered, I could see bodies passing by the window. It was so difficult to resist the urge to take one peek outside, as I am usually the party planner and amid any celebratory activity.

Oddly enough, I was not aware of the shower details and did not know if there was even a color scheme. I put on a jeweled pea-green strappy top and brown capris, and fifteen minutes before the guests were due to arrive, Paula brought me upstairs to see the setup and get situated. Imagine my surprise that both she and several friends were also wearing green and brown. These were the small things that brought me joy! They guided me into the dining room, where a corner table supported the most beautiful and majestic cake that I had ever seen, decorated with one brown face peeking out of the peapod. At that moment, it was as if the whole reality of losing Matthew hit me; I was now outside of the clinical settings of the doctor's visits and ultrasounds and was confronting the fact that we would only bring one child home. Have you ever been in a situation where you have experienced the juxtaposition of intense grief and intense gratitude? The love that had been poured into me with this celebration, combined with joy and hope of Mark fluttering in my uterus, exploded at that moment, and I wept. My tears flowed like a mighty river bursting forth from a dam that had been holding back pent-up sadness, disappointment, and pain. Yet, the release represented the power within the pain. I looked toward the possibilities with the renewed vigor of how this child and this experience would bring living water of hope, love, and joy to anyone we touched.

It is so important to remember that a process of positivity practices does not mean that we don't make space for sadness, disappointment, and the expression or release of these emotions. It's not either/or. It can be both/and.

I could sit with both feelings for a while, and then I had to choose what I would do next. I stepped into my joy tank and allowed myself to bathe in the love, prayers, and support that the women in my community were showering on me that afternoon.

Refilling My Joy Tank

I admit that I was somewhat relieved that the plan was for me to deliver by C-section. First, as a urologist, I see the leaky, dropping bladders that can develop years after vaginal deliveries. Second, the traumatic memories of severe menstrual cramps stayed with me, and I wasn't looking forward to dealing with contractions. So, when I started having intense abdominal and pelvic pain on Sunday, June 25ᵗʰ, 2006, I was scared and indignant. I was scared because I was two days shy of 32 weeks, too early for Mark to be born. I had been praying that we would make it to at least 34 weeks. I was scared because I was worried about whether my uterus would rupture from the intense contractions because of my previous fibroid surgeries. Indignant because I wasn't supposed to experience labor pains!

I remember calling my obstetrician, who thought I was having the same type of Braxton Hicks contractions (sporadic uterine contractions that typically occur in the second and third trimester of pregnancy) I had been having for months. But this felt different. I always encourage my patients to be attuned to their bodies so that when something feels different, no one can talk you out of getting it checked out. We packed up and trudged over to our community hospital, and sure enough, I was in premature labor. The community hospital did not have the facilities to take care of babies born before thirty-four weeks, so I was transferred to one of the leading Harvard Hospitals. I had never met the covering high-risk obstetrician at the premier hospital. Initially, I was managed by the residents who were communicating by phone with my high-risk obstetrician. I prayed that they could slow down my labor so that Mark would have a few more weeks inside. That was not to be. The doctors told me I was at high risk of developing an infection, and it was safer to deliver Mark while he was infection-free than keep him inside and have him become sick. We had no choice, and I delivered by C-section, performed by the covering high-risk OB doctor.

I found myself in a situation that many of my patients deal with every day. I had a doctor who had been following me for months and who knew everything about me. We had developed a relationship. I trusted him, and we had been through highs and lows together. And now, here I was at a different hospital, being treated by a team who did not know me, and it was an unsettling feeling. I knew the system had measures in place for the information about my history to be available in the medical records. I knew these doctors were competent, but the irrational, human part of me wanted the person who had been caring for me the entire time to be by my side.

Twelve hours elapsed between the time I arrived at the premier hospital and the C-section. Twelve hours of agony with conversations about delayed delivery risks because of the possibility of infection to Mark. Agonizing because the exams to determine what was happening with my cervix were extremely painful. Agonizing because the pain from the contractions paled compared to the pain in my heart. I wanted to have an epidural placed to delay the delivery. I was still trying to exert control. I was holding on, and God was turning the limit on the opportunity for me to trust Him more. "Let go! I haven't brought you this far to leave you now. You are surrounded by doctors who know what they are doing. Let go!" I had been stripped down, and had no choice but to stop fighting. Then, I had to make a decision that I had been putting off —whether I would see and hold our dead son, Matthew. I wrestled with the guilt of not planning to hold him and honor him in death, but the pain of seeing his body that way seemed unimaginable, and I reached to God for answers. I cried and cried and prayed and prayed and eventually knew that I did not want my son's last image to be his lifeless body. And God said, "It's okay. You honor him in your heart, where he will live on forever."

We finally delivered our little warrior and his protector. Mark was delivered first, and I held him briefly before they whisked him off to the NICU. I closed my eyes and prayed as they delivered Matthew, and Charles held him. As the priest blessed him and baptized him as Matthew Charles Anderson, my heart felt as if it had shattered into a million pieces. Then I had to pick up the pieces and put them back together. I had to claw my way up the mountain of fear and grief and see, as I crested the top, that for all the hardship and pain, we had a son who was alive at that moment. I finally had the chance to be a mother. I would exercise HOP #2, Convert a limit into an opportunity, and be the best mother I could be. That started with converting any negative energy into positive energy and vibes and sending those Mark's way with prayers of safety and protection in the NICU.

There is a space between simultaneous grief and relief that is difficult to describe. It manifests as paroxysms of crying— happy and sad tears—moments of chest-clutching longing for what could have been, and exhilaration for the miracle lying in your arms. It is waking up in the middle of the night with a feeling of emptiness but being filled up by the nurse's midnight call from the neonatal nursery, where Mark spent the first four weeks of his life, with the report that his weight had increased by two grams from the previous day. These small wins eased the pain and fear of loss and refilled my Joy Tank.

Replacing Fear with Gratitude

A few days after I had delivered, my ankles swelled slightly. I dismissed this as a typical postpartum change, especially since I had had a C-section and had been on my feet a lot, running back and forth to the hospital to see Mark. There was no pain, and both ankles were affected. Frankly, I was so focused on Mark and his well-being that I gave little thought to anything else. How often have you found yourself in a situation where a child or loved one was ill, and your singular focus becomes caring for that person? I was consumed with Mark. I was obsessed with doing as much skin-to-skin contact as I could, tracking how much he was drinking, checking middle-of-the-night weights, and watching his heart rate and breathing like a hawk. It was as if I were pouring my very life into his.

A week before Mark came home, the house was buzzing with family members making ready for his arrival, and my mother-in-law asked me, "What's wrong with your eye?"

Puzzled, I looked in the mirror. It appeared as if someone had thrown a red paintball into my eyes. The doctor in me kicked in, and I immediately checked my blood pressure, 180/100. There began a bumpy journey of what was preeclampsia but not well understood in this post-delivery state. At that point, I don't even think I knew that Black maternal mortality was three to four times higher than White maternal mortality. My blood pressure was so labile that it would go up at the drop of a hat. The increase seemed to be connected to breastfeeding, and it felt as if I was getting no significant help from my doctors.

I was caught up in the crosshairs of medicine, which is especially common in major hospital systems and can result in disjointed follow-up, a series of handoffs, and an unclear chain of responsibility. A general obstetrician initially followed me. I was referred to a high-risk obstetrician after the first trimester because I was over 35 and pregnant with twins. Dr. Hall, who saw patients at one of the subsidiary community hospitals associated with the leading Harvard Hospitals, followed the boys' progress and did all the high-level prenatal testing. My regular OB was also at that community hospital. The plan was to perform a scheduled C-section when I was 36 weeks because I had prior fibroid surgery, which made my uterus weak in some areas that could rupture if I went into labor.

Once I was discharged from the hospital, I was instructed to call for a follow-up appointment with my regular OB. He had not performed the C-section, so he was disconnected from the process. When I started having blood pressure (BP) issues, my doctors played musical chairs. I was directed from my high-risk OB to my regular OB to my PCP. Thankfully, I was persistent, but I can quickly see how frustrating this is for new mothers who don't know how to advocate for themselves. When I saw my PCP, she recommended seeing a hypertension specialist to rule out other causes because my BP was so high and did not seem to fit the picture of preeclampsia, which usually occurs predelivery. I now had a good glimpse of how patients feel when they come in to see us doctors with a problem that no one seems to understand. It can be the most deflating and hopeless kind of feeling. None of the doctors understood why my blood pressure was high *after* I had the baby when it was perfectly fine during the pregnancy. Most of the time, because my BP was not significantly elevated in the office, the doctors thought I was hysterical when I reported how high my BP would rise. They suggested that I made myself so anxious that it was creating a vicious cycle with my blood pressure. Perhaps if I had had a doctor who had seen a large volume of Black patients, the diagnosis would have been clear.

I was a wreck. It is scary to be a doctor and know the possible outcomes of my physical signs and symptoms. Negativity had me in a vice grip, and I was down the path of not only the fear of having a stroke but also the terrifying thought of all the other catastrophes that hypertension can cause, like kidney failure and heart failure. I was obsessed with checking my blood pressure, and the more I checked, the higher it became. Has that ever happened to you? I was popping pills left, right, and center. My husband would tell me to stop checking it, but I was caught up on a treadmill of fear from which I could not dismount. Negativity distracted me from focusing on the joy of being at home with our six-week-old Miracle Mark, and I had to shake myself and shift consciously. I had to focus on the process instead of the problem to get to the solution.

My husband and I started researching this pattern of elevated BP after pregnancy and found many reports on the American Heart Association website with similar issues made worse during breastfeeding. My doctor remained skeptical. I set up a schedule to monitor my BP and established clear criteria and symptoms that would cause me to check it outside the schedule. I was adjusting three different medications to control my BP. How many patients are equipped to do this? Very few. I vividly remember the day that the hypertension specialist finally believed me.

The exam room was tiny and quite dated. There were no windows, and I sat, facing the doctor, on a chair wedged next to her small desk. The exam table crowded the other wall, barely leaving enough space to walk by it to the desk. Dr. May regarded me with her pale blue eyes—eyes that seemed to look beyond me into the distance, even though the room was the size of a closet! I wondered if she remembered I was a surgeon, even though that shouldn't matter. Somehow, I didn't feel the sense of collegiality, kinship, or even warmth that I usually extend to the physicians I care for. Her nasal voice made a case for why things were not as bad as I had been describing, as none of the studies supported what I had reported. I could feel my blood pressure rising as she spoke to me. First, I felt an intensely nauseous sensation in the pit of my stomach, and then it was as if someone had punched me in the gut. At that exact moment, she asked me to sit on the table to examine me. She started by taking my blood pressure. I could feel my head swirling, and I was scared. As I gazed intently at her face and the dial of the blood pressure cuff inched up and up, I saw the change in her expression from nonchalant and distant to mirroring my fear. Her voice became a few octaves higher as she asked how I was feeling.

"The same way I always feel when my blood pressure is high," I replied.

My blood pressure had become dangerously high in a matter of minutes, and now she could see firsthand what I had been talking about. She immediately called 911. To add insult to injury, the EMTs were upset that they were being called for such a quick trip as the doctor's office was just across the street from the hospital. My blood pressure was dangerously elevated and the safest way to transport me was by ambulance. They didn't care about that detail; I was not a patient to them. I was an inconvenience. It was as if I was invisible. They bickered and complained the entire time and never seemed to be in the least bit concerned about the fact that I could have a stroke. It was as if my life didn't matter, and I was not worthy of them doing their jobs. I had to put my hands up and turn away from anger. "Not today, anger! Not today." You will not run up my blood pressure even more. It is difficult to do this. I had to close my eyes and focus on being thankful that the hospital was merely a stone's throw away and concentrate on taking deep breaths. *Don't let these fools get under your skin,* I kept telling myself.

I am thankful to be alive today, unlike many professional Black women who became maternal mortality statistics. I was attuned that something problematic was happening in my body, and I knew the actual risks of having severely elevated blood pressure. Because I was a doctor, I had the following advantages:

- I knew immediately when my mother-in-law saw my eye that I needed to check my BP.

- I had a blood pressure cuff at home.

- I did not give up until I had appointments with the appropriate doctor, despite getting punted from place to place.

- I knew enough not to accept banal reassurances without having good explanations.

- I was insistent about what symptoms I was experiencing, even if they could not appreciate them when I was in the office.

- I was confident and knowledgeable enough to adjust medications in real-time; otherwise, I would have had times of significantly sustained elevated blood pressure, which could have led to catastrophic issues.

- I was confident in navigating research and the system to apply my critical thinking to self-diagnosing (most of the time, this is not a good practice for doctors, but I had no choice).

I had access to more information and knowledge than many African American women, but my experience as a pregnant Black woman is still sadly one of the statistics. There were many revelations in this experience and, despite how gut-wrenching it was, I could still step back and apply HOP #2: Convert a limit into an opportunity!

I found an opportunity to be thankful. I understood that Matthew had provided protection not only for Mark but also for me. It was as if he gave his life for both of us. Had I continued to carry both live twins, I would likely have had a severe preeclampsia case during pregnancy, and my blood pressure would have been worse. The sense of gratitude was overwhelming, and I could experience joy amid the pain. All I had to do was squeeze the positivity hose's nozzle connected to my full Joy Tank. The hose was there; I just had to choose to turn on the access to the resource. All things work together for good.

The "Opportunity" for a Deeper Family Connection

My fertility journey had been so arduous and complicated that I figured I had one shot. When we became pregnant with twins, I was overjoyed. I knew firsthand the joy and luxury of a built-in buddy. For this to be a one-and-done for me was remarkable. The romantic visions of matching boy outfits, family trips—one boy for me, one boy for Charles—double strollers, and twin festivals, filled me with delight. But that wasn't to be. Instead, God had a miracle in another womb. Three months after I conceived, my twin brother, Hubert's wife became pregnant. Their son, Lucas, was delivered four months after Matthew and Mark were born. His name continued the theme of the Gospels of the New Testament. Lucas and Mark have grown up almost like twins. Our families are incredibly close, and we are raising our boys together with a preordained bond. The limit of Matthew's loss manifested an opportunity for two families to come together in ways that created so much joy.

God's perfect plan for love, joy, and peace in our lives never fails. For many years, my mother wondered whether she would ever have any grandchildren. Finally, in 2006, within four months, she would coddle two newborn grandsons. Four years later, Jacob, Lucas's brother, was born. The "Brozins" (cousins but like brothers), so close in age, now gather at her feet. Her passion for education still courses through her veins, igniting a love of learning in her grandsons. She delights in their every silly remark, new discoveries, non-stop questions and is responsible for the foundation of their academic excellence. Gran-Gran's home became an Island of Positivity and a hub of educational exploration for the "Brozins" and their friends on Sunday afternoons and during school vacations. Her perpetual excitement about teaching them, in addition to her skill and commitment to the fundamentals of learning, has yielded young scholars and boys who embrace her old-school discipline with good humor. She bubbles over with optimism, and the boys frequently enact Gran-Gran isms which are hilarious. I sometimes look at the three boys gathered and wonder what it would have been like if Matthew was there with them, and I get teary-eyed for a moment. But the prolonged tears that I cannot contain are those of joy as I gaze upon Gran-Gran and her grandsons. I am reminded that in the middle of adverse situations, when we cannot imagine that we can ever find our joy, just hold on. Bit by bit, our fingers will find their way to the Positivity hose nozzles of our unlimited tank of joy, and we just have to choose to squeeze.

Writing as Healing

My writing has become a healing source in ways that I did not even understand. I was inspired to write before becoming pregnant because the lack of strong, positive, diverse female characters in children's books dismayed me. After the dust settled, that desire grew stronger and stronger, and Dr. Dee Dee Dynamo, Girl Super Surgeon, was born. She was a part of me, an expression of my GPS manifest in physical form. It was as if she became my child. I remember waiting for my first book, *Mission to Pluto,* to arrive feeling as if I had given birth when I saw Dr. Dee Dee's beautiful eyes staring back at me from the cover.

In my second book, *Meteorite Mission,* Dr. Dee Dee Dynamo is summoned to Chelyabinsk, Russia, because there is a meteorite collision and people are hurt. Matty Meteorite, the son, broke loose from Astrid Asteroid, the mom, and created a huge crash and loads of confusion in Chelyabinsk, Russia. At the end of the story, Matty Meteorite is reconstructed by Dr. Dee Dynamo and reunited with his mom, Astrid Asteroid.

Like Matty Meteorite and Astrid, Matthew was a part of me. His impact on my life was Earth-shattering, leaving an enormous crater in my heart in those short moments. Without even knowing it, I had written a story that served as a channel and outlet for my pain as beautiful, expressive art. I had effectively exercised HOP #2: Convert a limit into an opportunity!

The limit of Matthew's loss had created the opportunity for me to write a story that blessed many kids and me. The work of turning on the Positivity Hoses from my Joy Tank has been so worth it, as that crater is now filled with love, hope, joy, peace, and acceptance. I believe that, like Matty and Astrid, at the end of our earthly story, Matthew, Mark, and I will be reunited.

Finding Joy in Practicing Medicine Again

I took a year off after delivering the boys. I needed time to savor Mark and to bond, as well as give myself the space to experience a wide range of emotions that occur in the cramped space framed by unspeakable joy and heartbreaking grief. As physicians, we give up so much in our pursuit of medicine.

We sacrifice ourselves in the service to others. We often put ourselves and our families last as we meet the obligations and responsibilities that we swore to uphold in the Hippocratic Oath, "Do no harm." My pledge emanated from the depths of my soul. I honestly didn't understand that the oath needed to first apply to me to be whole and healthy in order to care for others wholeheartedly. I needed time to care for myself and my son before reactivating the Joy Tank hoses when practicing medicine.

Sometimes, after one has sustained trauma, that experience takes up such prominence in your mind that you forget the joys of what life was like before the trauma. I needed to reconnect to my *why,* which lived in my Joy Tank. I thought of some of my patients. I just love elderly patients. I love listening to their stories; I love looking into their deeply lined faces and following the paths of wisdom coursing across their cheeks. I love their humor and how they laugh at themselves and don't sweat the small stuff. And I love the joy that they exude every day. I love finding creative ways to explain the problem and the options to my patients, even as they dig their heels in, and I have to coax them gently and patiently into trying something new.

UROLOGY STORY:
LOVE MARRIED TO SACRIFICE BIRTHS JOY

When I started in private practice, I inherited Mrs. Soul, who had been having her urethra stretched for years. This was the old way of treating urinary urgency, frequency, and recurrent urinary tract infections, resulting in scarring of the urethra. The procedure was excruciating, and I would almost be in tears as I apologized and gradually cranked up the barbaric dilation device. Despite the pain, Mrs. Soul would be upbeat and reassure me she was a tough cookie.

One day Mrs. Soul came in on her 60th wedding anniversary, and I playfully asked whether she and her husband would be "getting busy" later on. She giggled mischievously and said to me that one of the secrets to a good marriage was both people being on the same page related to their sex life. She said that the little blue pill had made life difficult for older women like her who had dryness and narrowing of the vagina, causing pain with intercourse. But her husband, who was legally blind, insisted that he must take the blue pill to have his weekly fix. So, Mrs. Soul substituted the little blue pill with a sugar pill, which she faithfully dispensed once a week. Every week he got into the throes of passion as he slapped against her knee, far from the intended target! Mrs. Soul provided the appropriate sound effects! He was happy, and she was happy! She had turned on her Joy Tank hoses, activated a solution and converted both of their limits into an opportunity that met both of their needs.

Oh, how we would laugh every month when she visited as we skipped in the puddles that her overflowing Joy Tank created on the floor. Those simple times of connecting to joy during that visit made the visit's pain recede into the background. These memories helped me turn back on the hoses of my Joy Tank in the practice of medicine.

Do you know joy is a part of your birthright? It is an eternal promise inherent in your very existence. Do you know joy lives in every cell and cannot be extricated from the core of who you are? Do you know joy is not a feeling but a state of being? How often do you interchange happiness and joy? What if you had the unyielding belief that your joy is always present and you can develop the skill to tap into it? How much more confidently would you approach the tough times in your life? How often do you hear the saying, "I will not let them steal my joy?" Your joy is in an impenetrable, top security tank, overflowing onto the world. It is in every cell of your body, so no one can separate you from it! You can share your joy, but no one can steal it!

POSITIVITY PAUSE

Redefine, Recharge, Reset, Resume- How can you find joy when you are staring down the barrel of devastating circumstances? It simply starts with an understanding of what joy is. Often, we confuse happiness, the feel-good emotion related to external circumstances, and joy. Joy is the inner sense of well-being that is selfless and connects you to something bigger than yourself. You have a divine and infinite supply, an unlimited reservoir, a Joy Tank. Even when the external circumstances cloak you in despair and cause unhappiness and sorrow at man's inhumanity to man, you can remain anchored in joy. Thinking about the Habits of Positivity as those access points to our joy, combined with the active choice to turn on the hoses, reminds us we have access to everything we need to launch our internal S.U.P.E.R. powers. We just have to understand how to access and then turn them on.

Our Joy Tank is never depleted. We function from a place of overflow, which touches those around us. Operating from this place of an unlimited reservoir positions us to function from a place of abundance rather than lack. It makes us excited to turn on our Positivity Hoses and impact the world. Think of how the fires of discrimination, racism, misogyny, and xenophobia were started by limited thinking. Say "Not today" to limited thinking and extinguish those fires by opening your Positivity Hoses and spraying joy everywhere. You can do it, and you can teach your kids to do it. This is how you deactivate limited thinking and negativity!

POSITIVITY PRACTICE

Access Your Joy Tank

1. Meditate on what your Joy Tank looks like. What is in it?

2. Draw or create it and attach the Positivity Hoses.

3. What are some experiences that clog your Joy Tank hoses?

4. Reflect on experiences where you accessed your Joy Tank.

5. Sit for 10 minutes every day and reflect on an experience during the day when it seemed as if you could not get into your Joy Tank. Turn on each of the Habits of Positivity Hoses and then journal how it became easier.

TRANSFORMATION

Reflect on the differences between when you were unaware that you had a Joy Tank that is always full versus how you feel now that you know how to unclog the hoses to your tank, and journal your responses below:

Before I started thinking about my Joy Tank as always available to me and I just needed to learn how to activate my Positivity Hoses, I used to feel:

Now that I think about my Joy Tank daily and have become skilled at cleaning out my hoses and turning them on I feel:

HABIT OF POSITIVITY #3

Keep the Positive;
Discard the Negative!

CHAPTER 6

Unlimited Peace—
Life Pendulum

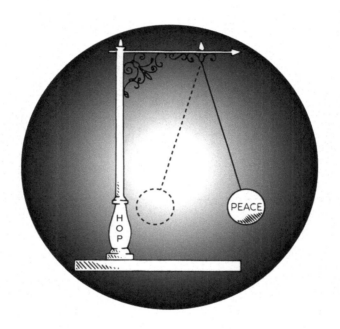

"Be anxious for nothing, but in everything by prayer and supplication, with thanksgiving, let your requests be known to God; and the PEACE of God which surpasses all understanding will guard your hearts and minds through Christ Jesus."

—PHILIPPIANS 4:6-7

> *"Make no mistake, all of the success, abundance and PEACE you desire comes from knowing your spirit deeply and intimately. "*
>
> **—OPRAH**

NOT BY MY STRENGTH BUT yours, Lord. How many times have you reflected on situations and wondered how you endured? Or contemplated the task in front of you and didn't think you had what it took to succeed? How many times have you felt as if your life sometimes seems to swing from one extreme to another, shattering your peace? Do you know that our kids are plagued with the same feelings, especially in this age of social media? This is yet another strategy of the negativity terrorist to hijack our peace. How do you gain control, restore your peace and help your kids to regain theirs? By declaring, "Not today, hijacker, not today!"

Depending upon our circumstances, our Life Pendulum swings toward Positivity or away from Positivity. And life is always going to swing. The year 2020 has taught us about how the swing can be unexpected. We all have a positive center. It's there, at our core, and we have access to it. We can use the Habits of Positivity as our center to help keep us balanced. Focusing on the positives and discarding the negatives can move your Life Pendulum toward the center so that you experience more peace.

Keeping the Positive in the Arc of the Pendulum

I often wonder how I made it through my surgical training. It comprised long, grueling hours, loads of information crammed into my head, multiple challenges, and few people who looked like me. But fifteen years after high school, I marched across the threshold into urologic surgery adulthood! I could start doing all the things I had trained for and pay down some bills and school debt. There were countless difficulties, but there were also good times, lots of laughs, triumphs, people who believed in me, and the feeling of joy as I cared for patients, reminding me of why I went into urology. As I crossed the threshold as a fully trained urologic surgeon, I knew that I would have to hold fast to HOP #3: Keep the positives; Discard the negatives.

I joined a three-person practice just south of Boston, where the founding partner had just retired. Of course, I was a unicorn, but despite that, the first few years were smooth. I was super busy. I loved my patients, and I was operating like crazy. During residency, I had tried to be "one of the guys." I had convinced myself that if I showed up to do the work the same as everyone else, I'd be okay. So, I denied certain parts of myself, like starting a family, because I needed to pull my weight. A common belief is that when female residents become pregnant, someone else would have to do their work, and there is a stigma attached to that.

I began private practice with the same mentality. A year after I started, one of the male partners retired, and yet again, I delayed starting a family. I did not want to burden the remaining partners with the clinical and on-call responsibilities. I had been so conditioned in this mode of thinking that I was more concerned about caring for their needs than I was about caring for mine. I tried to disprove the commonly held male belief and stereotype about why women didn't belong in surgery, so I waited until we added another partner. All seemed well in paradise. I remember going to the Women in Urology conference and hearing all the horror stories about women having discriminatory experiences in their practices and feeling blessed that my practice was different.

My two male partners were ten years apart in age. The older partner was in his early fifties and was the epitome of a provincial surgeon. He was a New England boy, a creature of habit. His routine was cast in concrete. He worked out at the same gym on the same days for the twenty years he had been in practice. He played tennis at the same times, with the same people, and his wife kept his same desk drawer stocked with the same snacks and his favorite soda, Pepsi. He was a gentleman, kind and paternal. I would venture to say that he had never worked with a Black female surgeon.

The other partner had an interesting character. He would always look at me with an expression that vacillated between bemusement and fascination as he tried to figure out the logic of how I had gained my pedigree! How was I working shoulder to shoulder with him? He would question me as if searching for some inconsistency or elusive answer that would align with his worldview. He was probably most comfortable simply pretending that I didn't exist, which became apparent to me years later after I left the practice. We would see each other at meetings, and he would look right through me even though we had worked together for seven years. After I recognized what was happening, I would put my hand up whenever I saw him, and mutter "Not today," and I would look right through him, too!

I'm sure many of you have had similar experiences when it seems as if you have been rendered invisible. A colleague, coworker, or acquaintance walks by you as if he/she did not see you, and you know that he/she did because you observed him/her as he/she looked your way and then looked away. You have three choices in those situations:

- Sometimes, you just don't feel like being bothered, so you keep moving and don't give it a second thought.

- If the situation occurs repeatedly, you conclude that this is not your issue, and there is no need to assign any significance to this person's behavior. Consciously discard the negative energy and realize that he/she does not belong in your universe and therefore cannot cause your pendulum to swing too far away from your center of positivity. Thus, you keep your peace.

- Extend the benefit of the doubt. Maybe he/she didn't see you, so you shorten the swing of your Life Pendulum away from positivity and quickly reverse direction, swinging back toward positivity and greet that person. Every so often, the greeting may require you to be dramatic.

I make these choices almost daily. For example, one morning, I cruised into the doctor's lounge before the start of my surgery to grab a snack. The countertops were jam-packed with high-carb goodies, such as doughnuts, the staple peanut butter and jelly, a fruit bowl for the healthy option, and the requisite Keurig machine. There were two doctors in the rather intimate lounge, a white male anesthesiologist with whom I worked periodically, and an Indian radiologist.

"Good morning, gentlemen," I said, to which neither of them responded. So, I stopped right beside them, and I repeated, "Good morning, gentlemen."

The radiologist stopped speaking, looked over at me, and said, "Good morning, Dr. Williams."

Meanwhile, the anesthesiologist who stood facing the radiologist, less than three feet from me, said absolutely nothing. So, I said "Not today" to feeling invisible and insignificant. I would not allow this situation to swing my pendulum to the extreme and play the disrespect over and over in my head for the rest of the day, fixated on what I should have said. So, I inserted myself in between the two men, facing the anesthesiologist— my head barely at the level of his chest—and I reached up, placing both of my hands on either side of his face, the way you do when trying to get a child's attention. I gently directed his face down until we made eye contact, and I said again, "Good morning."

It was almost as if I had lit his tail on fire! He was so startled that he almost jumped out of his skin and spluttered, "Good morning, Dr. Williams! I didn't even see you."

I thought to myself, *I know, but now you do!* I chuckled all day long, and you can bet I never had this issue with him again! I had jolted him out of whatever unconscious bias he had that made me invisible to him; sometimes, it just takes a jolt to expose those biases.

For the first three years of practice, life felt rather good. I disguised my ovaries, masqueraded as a guy, and all was well, especially if I ignored the younger partner's confused look. We had the same number of workdays, clinic sessions, and operating room time, each having every other Friday off. I was making money, taking vacations, hanging out with family, and was more active in my community—life was good! There was some downtime in our schedule during which my male partners would mostly go to the gym or swim, but as I was not a part of that "old boys club," I generally went shopping! I was not "other," but I was different, and no disguising could change that! I felt comfortable in my skin.

After three years, the practice hired a new urologist, and I was now officially a partner. Finally, it was time to start a family, so I eliminated all the nonproductive downtime and changed my schedule to work four days a week. Nothing changed in my operating room commitments, clinic shifts, or my on-call responsibilities, but I "worked" half a day less per week than my partners. Essentially, the half-day that they were working out or playing tennis, I decided I wanted to use it for my chosen activities. I did not have free sessions to swim or play tennis during the day. When I was at work, I was focused and productive, and my volume and revenue reflected my efforts. I was the second-highest in revenue generated for the practice. Suddenly, I had changed the script and drawn attention to my differences. I would not have predicted the ire that this created for my partners.

Have you ever broken the mold of expectations and stepped into your uniqueness? All hell breaks loose, and resistance to differentiation occurs. As long as I was doing the same thing as my partners, they could ignore my differences and shelter comfortably and conveniently in our commonality. As soon as I stepped outside of the box, they could no longer overlook I was female. What is a typical response when something makes us uncomfortable or introduces change? Discredit! Devalue! Cut down to size and force back into the box! But I was not having it. "Not today!"

For each punch, I had a block and counterpunch. It was exhausting. Initially, with each incident, I felt myself swinging long arcs from one extreme of the pendulum to the other through all kinds of negative emotions. There would be crazy things like them wanting to change our compensation metric to reflect the free time when we were available to help each other, rather than revenue generated or hours worked! As ludicrous as it sounds, it was a foreshadowing of a current political phenomenon. Create a new norm with a left-field, ludicrous perspective and believe its reasonableness so strongly that it's impossible to have a rational conversation. I realized I was enlisting HOP #3—Keep the positive; Discard the negative—quick, fast, and in a hurry and applying it to the swing of the pendulum of emotion, anger, disappointment, annoyance, and irritation. As I focused on keeping the Habits of Positivity at the center, the arc of the swing became smaller, and I could have more access to unlimited peace.

Unlimited Peace Resides at the Center of My Life Pendulum

One way that we, as female physicians and busy professionals, abuse our bodies is that we squeeze in our medical care as an afterthought and never make ourselves a priority. My fertility process was no different. All the blood draws, tests, egg retrievals, transfers, and surgeries were plugged into hastily stolen moments from the clinic. After multiple stops and starts, we began our fourth cycle of IVF. I became pregnant with twin boys, and early bleeding relegated me to eight weeks of bedrest during the first trimester. I had a cerclage (ring around the cervix) placed as a precaution to prevent the cervix's early opening, and I returned to work. It was rough as I experienced chronic pelvic pain, pregnancy-related nausea and migraine headaches. As the twin pregnancy progressed and my body came under more and more duress, my doctors advised I decrease my work rigor. I held out for as long as I could because, as you may recall, I didn't want anyone to feel as if they were carrying my workload. But the time came when I had to capitulate for the sake of my boys, and I stopped taking call (being available to answer calls from the hospital or take care of emergencies).

The primary concern was not for my well-being but related to compensation. My "partners" wanted to ensure that I did not get what they surmised I didn't deserve, so they decreased my compensation because I could not take call. Have you ever been in a situation where you believed that you were on the battlefield fighting side by side with comrades, and when you fall, the same people—who you thought were fighting with you—kick you and step over you while you are on the ground? Then you know how I felt. Betrayed, disappointed, hurt. Also, unbeknownst to me, my "partners" had somehow deduced that based on the trajectory of my pregnancy and time off for maternity leave, I would not make enough to justify my "draw" (which is monies paid based on expected revenues). Imagine if you were making a considerable sacrifice to show up to work every day, despite being in emotional, mental, and physical pain, and on payday, everyone received a check but you? What would your first thought be? There must have been a mistake! That was mine, too. I immediately shuffled into our manager's office; a sweet woman, always smiling and was very kind to me.

"Oh, Jane," I said, "I just wanted to let you know there was a payroll error because I didn't get my paycheck today."

"I'm sorry, Dr. Williams," sincerity and embarrassment mixed in her voice, "Dr. Hill told me not to issue a paycheck to you."

"Wait, what? This was intentional?" I asked in disbelief.

It was as if someone had slapped me in the face with a towel soaked in sulfuric acid. Just consider. I'd had an inordinately difficult pregnancy after a long journey to get there, and these men showed no compassion or sensitivity. They didn't see me as a woman who could have been their sister, wife, or friend; they didn't see my humanity. They didn't respect me as a peer. Because of changes in my pregnancy, my high-risk obstetrician restricted my operating time. The practice's senior partner said, "If you can only tell us ahead of time, then we could plan." To say that he didn't get it would be generous. Somehow I kept getting the feeling that he thought I was deliberately disrupting the practice—that I was canceling patient visits and surgeries for kicks. Quite a few of my surgeries were booked jointly with other surgeons which had taken months to coordinate. Patients had made plans, taken time off of work, and I felt so guilty. There was no support, and I felt utterly alone. I wasn't one of the guys. I wasn't one of the girls. It seemed as if I wasn't deserving of the care and concern issued to others. I was a Black woman in an all-White male practice, and they saw me only as a workhorse.

Feeling as if I had knocked the wind out of my sails, I went home, crawled into bed, and just lay there trying to tame my emotions and find peace. My Life Pendulum was swinging wildly, and I had to get back to the center. As I lay there, I was transported back to my fourth year of medical school. I had decided that urology was going to be my specialty, and I was excited. My next step was to rotate through the urology departments in one of Boston's premier hospitals to have them get to know me and hopefully secure excellent grades and recommendation letters. My career depended on this. On one of my urology rotations, I was subjected to aggressive, condescending, blatantly insulting, and discriminatory behavior by my White male chief resident and White male OR nurse. The nurse pushed me out of the way and screamed at me to leave the OR because he assumed I was some support worker who did not belong in the room. I was so angry and unsettled that I questioned if I even wanted to be a urologist. Thankfully, I had the VA experience to remind me why I had chosen this field, and I could focus on all the positives of my experiences. I could not allow these individuals to swing my pendulum so far away from my positivity center that I would end up giving up on my dream.

I was in a bind. Did I speak up and risk being blackballed and never matching in urology or just keep my mouth shut and forever carry that angst? I had to choose between writing a letter of complaint to the ombudsman at Harvard to report the discriminatory treatment or suck up the mistreatment and trade silence for an opportunity to pursue my dream. As my Life Pendulum swung wildly, driven by the fear of retaliation, I had to reach into the source of my unlimited peace. And there I found a deep knowing: *Do not be afraid.* And so, I spoke up. I did not apply to that program but had many other options, and I AM a urologic surgeon. I launched HOP #3—Keep the positive; Discard the negative—and didn't allow that experience to turn me away from urology. I took a risk to be seen and walk in my truth.

My mind shifted to my residency training as the first Black urology resident. I was fiery, marching to the beat of my drum, yet there were six male urologic surgeons under the leadership of Dr. John Libertino who made room for me to be me. They always made me feel as if I was 10 feet tall and served as mentors and advocates for me. I never doubted that they wanted the best for me. These were the positive experiences that I could place on my life scales to shift from the very hurtful experience within my practice.

And as I lay in that bed, pregnant with our twins, I had to reach down to that same unlimited peace that I had found during medical school. I had to visualize my Life Pendulum with the Habits of Positivity as the center and hold fast to my source of unlimited peace so that my male colleagues could not swing me to extremes. The following morning, I said "Not today" to being an unappreciated workhorse. I canceled my clinics and surgical cases for the rest of the week. I challenged the "partners," who could not seem to grasp why I was so upset. They lacked empathy and could not for a moment take a step back to see how their actions would compound my stress. My compensation was reinstated, but that experience left me with a bitter taste in my mouth. At six months, we lost one of our twin sons. I was devastated, but desperately held onto the hand of the one who offers us unlimited peace. I knew that I could never go back to that practice. My obstetrician placed me on bed rest for the rest of my pregnancy. Did the stress of the practice contribute to that loss? We know that stress is one factor attributed to the disproportionately elevated rates of Black maternal mortality and infant mortality.

When the Life Pendulum Swings Toward Grief

How do we cope and hope during personal loss when it seems as if the pendulum of life is swinging to such an extreme that there is no end in sight? Where do you find peace? Whether it is the loss of a treasured friendship because of death or just a severe change in life circumstances, the grief you experience may feel never-ending. That is what it felt like when we lost my husband's best friend, Gary, to COVID-19 on March 29th, 2020.

I first met Gary 35 years ago when he visited my then-boyfriend, Charles, at his Johns Hopkins Medical School townhouse. I heard him before I saw him! A loud, booming voice filled the entire townhouse; I nervously inched down the stairs. This was a huge moment! Even though it was not expressly stated, I knew it was important to Charles that Gary like me. They met in 1979 at Princeton University, and Charles and Gary had been best friends since the first week of freshman year. As I stepped on the bottom stair, I was swept up in the biggest bear hug ever, and Gary had been my most ardent fan since. While at Princeton, everyone knew Charles and Gary. They were the Sonic Sounds Production DJ crew, so it is not surprising that Gary became a New York entertainment lawyer with his own record label. It was a fast life, and I did a lot of nail-biting whenever Charles visited. The friendship was unshakeable, and the annual BFF reunion between Charles and Gary happened every August on the same wooden bench facing the famed Martha's Vineyard Inkwell Beach.

Gary had grown up spending summers on the Vineyard, and like a homing pigeon, he was programmed to return to base. Oak Bluffs was his destination when he hastily packed up his soon-to-be wife and son and joined the other New Yorkers escaping the brutal onslaught of COVID-19 on the Big Apple. In his inimitable fashion, as he stood in the ferry line, he caught the attention of a *Boston Globe* reporter who quoted Gary Jenkins Esq. in a March 18th, 2020 article as planning to "sit on my front porch, smoke a cigar and not see anyone." Five days after arriving on the Island, he married the love of his life. The day after they tied the knot, he fainted, was diagnosed with COVID-19 and bilateral pneumonia, and traveled back to New York City to be admitted to New York-Presbyterian Hospital.

Gary was penning text updates in his upbeat, tongue-in-cheek style. With supplemental oxygen to support his breathing, he joked that we doctors had been holding out on him about how an oxygen "high" could feel so good! Within 24 hours, with oxygen requirements increasing, Gary texted to say that doctors would place the breathing tube for a few days, and he would chat with us thereafter. Within the subsequent 24 hours, COVID-19 ravaged Gary's kidneys and lungs, and his heart failed five days later on Sunday, March 29th. Gary had just turned 57 and was one of the first thousand people in the US to die of COVID-19.

Gary told Charles, "If this is God's will for me, I am at peace with it. I've lived a good life, and I know I will see my Pops, Doc. Anderson, and Jay." He had been very fond of Charles's dad (Doc. Anderson), and Jay was one of their best friends who died eight years earlier.

Gary acknowledged the seriousness of his condition, and those were among the last words he said to Charles. Yet when we received the call, it seemed so surreal and so wrong. It was hard to fathom that in a matter of days, this larger-than-life force was gone, and the aftershock reverberated for days. We experienced a cycle of tears, unanswered questions, anger, extreme sadness, and denial. Old photos, classic DJ mixed tapes and relived highlights over the years caused the memories and tears to flood even more. It seemed as if the waves of pain were intractable. How could we possibly pull any positivity from this situation? We had to declare, "Not today, hopelessness. Not today." Then, unexpectedly, laughter bubbled from within as the memories of outlandish experiences and escapades rose like a phoenix out of the ashes. The famous "Garyisms" surfaced and provided much comic relief, reminding us that the footprint that he left in our hearts was as vast as the Universe. Amid the sadness, we recognized that despite the loss, there were so many things we had kept that would be with us forever. We made room for those things and gave thanks for them. Gratitude and negative emotions cannot exist in the same place, and so our hopelessness was displaced in those moments. We were focused on HOP #3. Keep the positive; Discard the negative

The Sonic Sounds Production DJ crew was an indelible part of Charles' college and medical school experiences, but unlike Gary, he had discontinued spinning records as the demands of medicine took over. As he prepared for Gary's memorial service, listening to the old tapes reached down deep and touched a part of Charles' soul that had been buried for thirty years. Tentatively, he pulled out his iPad, loaded up a music app, and started mixing songs. It was as if the floodgates opened. Charles spent hours reconnecting with this art form that he had neglected, and the more time he spent, the more he seemed to walk a little more lightly and sleep a little more soundly. Within a week, he had mastered the new technology involved with mixing music, unearthed all of his signature songs and mixes, and declared that he could have a party. The beginning of the healing process from Gary's tragic loss resided in connecting to the essence of who Gary was in Charles' life and what they shared. The pendulum's swing shortened as the music allowed Charles to connect to the center filled with the positives that Gary brought to his life. He found peace there. Two weeks after Gary's memorial service, we held our first weekly virtual SocaMD Dance Party on the Island of Positivity. We created respite and took a Positivity Pause. We took time to put the pandemic blues, losses, worries, and fears on hold for a short while and revel in the legacy of love that Gary had left us. We shared that positive vibe with others, inviting them into the healing space that opens when we permit ourselves to shorten the pendulum's swing by focusing on the positives that remain, even when the person is no longer physically present. There were scores of friends and friends of friends who reached out to us after those beach parties to share that it blessed them immensely because of the respite provided amid the COVID-19 storm.

How many of you believe that being positive means that you deny that negativity exists? That is not true. Negativity is a part of life, but we get to call it out for what it is and restrict how dominant it becomes. Have you ever been in a negative spiral? How did it make you feel? Did you feel energized or completely depleted? How many of you would like to find your place of peace consciously? A tranquil place, free from disturbance? Life may not always permit us to stay in a place free from disturbance, but we can identify where that place is, how to get there, and actively pursue being there.

Thinking about your Life Pendulum with the Habits of Positivity as center creates a perspective that makes you less anxious when confronted with life's challenges because you believe that your experiences have a purpose.

You remain empowered even in the most disruptive circumstances. You are less likely to swing toward negative extremes, and you remain in the peace zone.

POSITIVITY PAUSE

Life is like a pendulum, swinging us from side to side. How we respond determines how far from the center the pendulum swings. The reassuring feature of our life's pendulum is that no matter how far away from the center we swing, there will always be a point where we will swing back through the center. The pendulum's central points are the Habits of Positivity that frame your responses and connect you to your internal S.U.P.E.R. powers.

Situations that swing away from your HOP center will always be a part of life. Life happens, and there is no escape. However, the pendulum's weight will pull you back to the center. By nature, we belong in a place of homeostasis and balance reflected in all of our life processes. We function best when we are centered. If you fully embrace the perspective that you can choose what that center is and acknowledge that life will always pull you back to that place, you are infused with calm when challenges arise. Choosing HOP as your center guarantees you will always experience the perspective that empowers you, no matter the situation. The question is: How much time do you spend in the center, experiencing the benefits of living from a place of positivity and unlimited peace?

If we choose negativity as our center, the forces of life will always pull us back there. There is power in declaring our center, as it defines our worldview and experience. Developing a discipline of choosing HOP as your center means that the pendulum's extreme swings become fewer and fewer, as your responses to situations reflect that center's overall perspective.

POSITIVITY PRACTICE

Activate Your Life Pendulum

1. Meditate on what your pendulum looks like?

2. How did your pendulum swing today?

3. Reflect on experiences where the swing was extreme. Why was it extreme?

4. Reflect on experiences where the swing was slight?

5. Sit for 10 minutes every day and think about your Life Pendulum and the experiences where the swing was extreme. Focus on your HOP center by applying the habits to each of the situations. List how the habits could have helped the swings be less extreme and made you feel more at peace and less anxious and worried.

TRANSFORMATION

Reflect on the differences when you didn't think about your Life Pendulum, the Habits of Positivity and the relationship to your peace versus how you feel now that you are more conscious of the arc of its swing of your Life Pendulum. Journal your responses below:

Before I started thinking about using the Habits of Positivity to control the swing of my Life Pendulum, I used to feel:

Now that I think about my Habits of Positivity as the center of my Life Pendulum daily and actively apply my habits to control the arc of the swing, I feel:

CHAPTER 7

Unlimited Forgiveness—
Life Scales

**"Love prospers when a fault is forgiven,
but dwelling on it separates close friends."**

—PROVERBS 17:9

> *"It's one of the greatest gifts you can give yourself, to FORGIVE. Forgive everybody."*
>
> **—MAYA ANGELO**

ARE THERE SITUATIONS WHERE YOU held on to hurt feelings that affect your relationship with those around you? Especially your children? How transformational would it be to let go and be free and light so that you can fully engage? When you change your world by shifting your thinking, it not only transforms how you experience your world—more confident, more joyful, more unencumbered—but also creates a new world for your children and generations to come.

Sometimes our Life Scales lean more toward positivity, and sometimes they lean more toward negativity, depending on our circumstances. When you incorporate HOP #3 into your life—Keep the positive; Discard the negative—your scales will weigh more heavily toward the positive. You will see in this chapter that a key ingredient for lightening the negativity load is forgiveness.

Angry feelings weigh us down, but when we can forgive those who have hurt us, we rebalance our Life Scales and free ourselves to feel more fulfilled, content, and happy.

Balancing My Life Scales with the Habits of Positivity

"You have a large mass in your chest," the rounding doctor said. I looked at the hands of the clock on the wall of the dimly lit hospital room, where I had spent the night torturously counting the minutes when I could go home to be with my newborn son. It was 7:00 a.m. on July 29th, 2006, when one of my worst fears as a physician was realized. The doctor's face was lined with concern, his gray hair neatly slicked down across a balding crown, a few wisps defying the hair gel. His kind eyes gazed steadily into mine, the shimmer of my tears reflecting his image.

My heart sank with a deep sense of letdown, like the breast milk that had soaked the front of my hospital gown. I had been hospitalized for severe postpartum hypertension and had no breast pump. In that instant, I knew I had become a casualty of the same system of care that I had trained in, trusted, and delivered every day to the best of my ability. But sh★t happens. I knew it. I had witnessed it. When it happens to you, a physician, at the hands of someone who trained you, whom you so admired that you sought them out when you needed surgery, it is devastating and brings you to your knees. After I had completed my silent, body-wracking, face-twisting cry, I looked into the conflicted face of the rounding doctor, who didn't know if he should brave the milky waterfall and comfort me or run for the hills.

With disappointment, fatigue, and sadness spilling from my lips, I responded, "I know what it is."

During my first year of medical school, my annual physical had identified an enlarged thyroid. The function was normal; we had a family history of enlarged thyroids, and I had no symptoms. Testing revealed a benign multinodular goiter, and the recommendation was to keep an eye on it. The goiter grew slowly and repeated biopsies over the years showed benign cells. During my second year of urology practice, a biopsy revealed a different cell type called Hurthle cells. These cells are only found in the thyroid and could be benign or cancerous. The only way to know for sure is to remove the thyroid. My thyroid was now so big that it was very visible, protruding from the base of my neck and pressing on my trachea.

Further testing pitched a curveball: A part of the thyroid was extending down into my chest. Now I was crazed and beside myself with worry. Did I have thyroid cancer? My life flashed before my eyes—I needed this mass out yesterday.

I immediately chose the thyroid surgeon at the hospital where I had completed some of my surgical training. I had observed his meticulousness and fastidiousness in the care of his patients, and I trusted him. He had been the brunt of many intern and resident jokes because of the dozens of little vascular clamps that adorned his neck like a stainless-steel necklace during the thyroid removal. No blood vessel would escape his scrutiny because post-op bleeding in the neck was dangerous. The surgeon and I met at length, reviewed all the radiologic and pathologic findings, and discussed the surgical plan.

The surgeon recommended I remove the entire thyroid, and the surgery went well. I recovered with no significant difficulties, and my pathology returned as a benign multinodular goiter with no Hurthle or cancer cells. I was thankful and ready to put that behind me and move on with the rest of my life. I started popping my thyroid replacement pill every day. I had seen so many patients who had had difficulty with thyroid regulation after surgery, but mine seemed to be a breeze. Oddly, I needed only an extremely low replacement dose, and everyone assumed it was because I was petite.

Fast forward eight years later, as I looked into the eyes of the doctor standing in front of me. I knew instantly, in that stomach-twisting, gut-wrenching, nauseated-to-my-core kind of way, that the thyroid surgeon had not removed the part of my thyroid that was growing into my chest. A review of his operative notes later revealed no mention of the thyroid part that had grown into my chest. There was no acknowledgment of its presence nor report of its removal.

I was livid. What if this had been cancerous? He would have left a large reservoir of cancer cells in my body. I would now need more surgery, which would mean time away from my son and work. It sucked. I returned to see him, mad as a hatter, and he was deeply apologetic. What do you do when one of your own fails you? I was part of the fraternity of physicians. Was I going to take some action against him? I just could not do it. I needed to actively employ HOP #3: Keep the positive; Discard the negative.

I could not go backward; I had to move forward. I needed to transform my anger and disappointment into gratitude and thank God that it was not cancer.

"What is the worst that could happen if I just left the mass as is?" I asked the surgeon.

Holy smokes! The cantaloupe-sized mass in my chest could spontaneously bleed, and if it did, I would not be able to breathe. I loved to travel. What if I was in the middle of some foreign land with limited health care? The thought made me dizzy. The mass needed to come out, and they would have to crack my chest to do it. I completely upended my Life Scales the way Jesus did in the temple. After I was done cussing, kicking, and screaming, I had to bend down, pick up the scales, and turn them right side up. I had to hold my hand up to the anger and unforgiveness that was threatening to consume me and say, "Not today!" I started by placing my Habits of Positivity on the scale, one habit at a time, starting with HOP #3—Keep the positive; Discard the negative—to help outweigh my negative situation on the other side. I had to keep stacking up my Habits of Positivity until the positives dominated.

Maybe there was some reason that I needed my native thyroid to help with my pregnancy with our son. Maybe the first surgeon was not experienced at removing the thyroid in the chest, and this was protection from some possible devastating complication.

The Scales of Forgiveness

I eventually had the second surgery when our son was six years old, and it was the most physically painful experience of my life. My Life Scales were in a significant state of imbalance, teeter-tottering toward anger, despair, and regret. Once again, I had to put my hand up to halt the negative flow of emotions by declaring, "Not today." I had to work to recreate balance. I could allow the heaviness of the situation to keep me weighed down, or I could acknowledge my feelings, express them, process them, and pile on the positivity weights, so I did not remain in the dumps.

I took two-and-a-half weeks off from work, which was utterly foolhardy! I had forgotten my redefinition of "super" back then and was trying to continue to show that somehow I was invincible. The surgery involved cutting my sternal bone. I could not turn my neck without pain for months; I could not drive, but yet I returned to work. What was I thinking?

My surgery was in November 2012, amid the last stages of trying to complete my first Dr. Dee Dee Dynamo book, *Mission to Pluto*. Despite the initial excruciating pain, the time away from work created the space for me to complete the book's revisions, released in February 2013. I could focus on the opportunity created by having the repeat surgery and claim the positives that resulted from the situation. If I had held on to the negatives of regret, anger, and disappointment, they would have continued to subtract from me, robbing me of my creativity and acting as a huge sinkhole. The situation would have weighed me down. I had to balance the scales. I had to forgive the original thyroid surgeon to not allow the weight of the negative feelings to displace the positives, which then made room for the good that came out of the situation. The transformation of understanding that follows forgiveness makes room for positivity, liberation, and freedom to fly. Unlimited forgiveness = unlimited flight.

UROLOGY STORY:
HELPING A PATIENT LET GO OF THE NEGATIVES

My personal experiences have allowed me to be more empathetic when patients have an adverse outcome from a surgical procedure. Surgery is always accompanied by risk, and unfortunately, complications do happen. In cases where the complication is unexpected, patients can feel overwhelmingly negative about the outcome and find it impossible to see any glimmer of positivity.

Being on-call can sometimes feel like a countdown, and this particular Sunday evening was no different. Even though I was thankful that it had been a quiet weekend, I still looked at my watch furtively, willing the time to go more quickly. Ordinarily, I would not have been on call that weekend, but one of my colleagues had asked me to switch. I had made a cardinal mistake, as one of the on-call rules is never to comment that it is quiet because that is an invitation for the floodgates to open. And so said, so done! My beeper rang five minutes after I had thanked my lucky stars that the weekend had been quiet. It was an emergency call from labor and delivery. Drats! That meant I was going to be at the hospital for a while. A patient who had failed to progress underwent an emergency C-section because the baby was in distress, and during delivery, the doctor had inadvertently cut into the bladder. When I entered the operating room, I could hear an audible sigh of relief from the staff.

"Dr. Williams, we're so glad you're on call," they said. I was the only female urologist in my group, and I dealt primarily with female issues. I scrubbed quickly, gowned and gloved, and stepped up to the OR table. There are times as a surgeon when the anatomy is so distorted that you have to pause to figure out where everything is located. Patience is a virtue, and I took my time getting everything sorted out and repairing the bladder. I wanted to repair the bladder and prevent the future possibility of urinary incontinence or fistulas between the bladder and vagina. Because of the location of the injury, I took meticulous care to decrease the likelihood of that complication. As the urologist in the group who did these types of surgeries most frequently, I was best qualified to achieve a great result.

Post-delivery, the patient was understandably devastated at the turn of events and sought to understand what had gone wrong. She had four previous deliveries of healthy sons that had all gone smoothly, and she struggled with the anger and bitterness that she had had to endure that experience. You see, this was the daughter that they had prayed for, and now her ability to fully enjoy the birth of her newborn daughter was clouded.

Over time, she never became incontinent and never developed a fistula to her bladder. Whenever she lamented about the experience, I would gently steer her back to the blessings and help her hold on to the positives and let go of the negatives. Her Life Scale could be balanced because her baby was healthy, and she had the best urologist to care for her that night, on a weekend when I was not even supposed to be on call. That was divine intervention! I could encourage her when she looked back at the experience to view it through the lens of HOP #3: Hold on to the positives and let go of any resentment that she harbored. She learned how to put the positives on the Life Scale and not allow the weight of the negatives to topple her scale.

How often do you try to achieve balance? This is a common aspiration in our lives, a mandate found on bumper stickers, in self-care courses, in devotional quotes. Can you think of the times when you have achieved balance? What has it felt like? Do you have the classic image of a trapeze artist walking on a tightrope? Highly skilled but teetering and subject to any shift that throws him or her off the rope? That feeling of instability and exposure goes against our desires for what balance represents. What if you think about balance differently? Rather than trying to walk a tightrope with the stress of never knowing what will knock you off the rope, you can instead choose what you place on the plates of your Life Scales. The focus is to declare that the positives will always outweigh the negatives and give weight to the things that matter. You also don't have to put everything on the scale simultaneously. Make conscious choices about what you place on your scale and always keep your Habits of Positivity as a constant presence on the scale. As you release the dead weight of unforgiveness and negativity, resistance evaporates, creating room for the things that fulfill, restore, and encourage you.

POSITIVITY PAUSE

Thinking about our lives as scales pays homage to the fact that life is a balancing act! Multiple situations are happening at the same time that requires choices, coordination, and multitasking. The scale suggests that things are constantly in motion, and as you place the various events and activities in your life on and off the scale, they will have inherently different weights. Some experiences will make you feel light, unfettered, and free, while others weigh you down. When negative events weigh down one side of your scale, you can set the intention of placing the Habits of Positivity on the other side to achieve emotional, mental, and physical balance. It is precisely for this reason that we must discard the negatives because they are heavy. However, the 5 Habits of Positivity will always create a balance that brings your Life Scales to equilibrium.

Take a breath and take stock of what is on your scale. Imagine the 5 Habits of Positivity on the scale. Feel the load ease as you intend to focus on the positives and take the negativity weights off.

POSITIVITY PRACTICE

Balance Your Life Scales

1. Meditate on what your Life Scales look like. What have you placed on them?

2. Draw your scales. Are they weighted more towards the positive or negative?

3. Reflect on experiences when it seemed as if your scales were weighed down by unforgiveness. What could you have done to tip the scales?

4. Reflect on experiences when you felt as if you countered unforgiveness' weight. Did your Habits of Positivity help?

5. Sit for 10 minutes every day and list the experiences during the day. Reflect on the experiences where the scales felt like negativity was weighing you down. Consider each Habit of Positivity and place it on the opposite side of the scales. Reflect on how this changed your perspective and shifted the balance of the scales towards a more positive outlook.

TRANSFORMATION

Reflect on the differences between when you thought little about balancing your Life Scales with the Habits of Positivity versus how you feel now that you are more conscious of focusing on the positives to help outweigh the negatives, and journal your responses below:

Before I started thinking about my Life Scales and using the Habits of Positivity to balance my experience, I used to feel:

Now that I think about my Life Scales daily and I actively place the Habits of Positivity on my scales I feel:

HABIT OF POSITIVITY #4

You are Unique with a Divine Purpose Linked to Caring for Others

CHAPTER 8

Unlimited Grace—
Life Slingshot

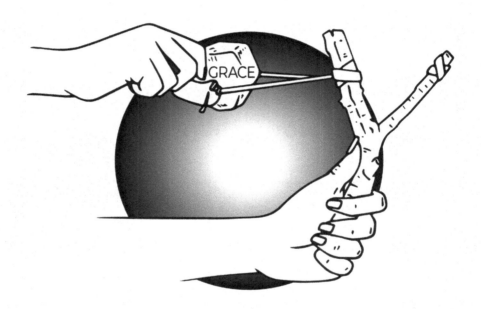

"For it is by GRACE you have been saved, through faith—and it is not from yourselves, it is a GIFT from God."

—EPHESIANS 2:8

"You are a slingshot, a catapult you are
Hitting targets near and far
You are powerful, you are meant to be
A force like no other, living intentionally."

—DR. ONEEKA WILLIAMS

HOW OFTEN DO YOU FIND yourself in a situation where someone pushes your buttons and grates on every last one of your nerves? Someone who irritates you beyond your wildest imagination, as if you were having hot pokers stuck in your eyes? Have you ever dealt with a bully or with someone who tries to thwart your every move? How do you respond? How do you guard against being sucked into a bottomless pit of negative emotions? How do you put your hand in his or her face and say "Not today" to aggravation, anger, and stress?

In this chapter, I will share some of my struggles with a former colleague with whom I clashed regularly, leaving me feeling frustrated, stressed, and depleted. I will show you how grace can be your best weapon in those infuriating situations and how you can load your Life Slingshot with the Habits of Positivity to replace anger and confrontation with calm communication and peace. Remembering that you are unique and have a divine purpose linked to caring for others (HOP

#4) can encourage you to respond with grace, which will help you cope, hope, and be well around challenging people.

Slinging Grace Instead of Anger

The relationship with the chief of my division was the bane of my existence. Our interactions were often tense, and it made my job more stressful. It was as if he made it his number one priority to diminish me because I would not fall in line. It was all about control. Have you ever encountered someone like this?

Dr. Weber arrived in 2008 with much fanfare. He was hired by a new CEO whose mission was to usher our system into the big business of medicine. According to one administrator, Dr. Weber was the LeBron James of the urology division- the star player. At the forefront of his field, he was a talented robotic surgeon who operated on royalty, dignitaries, CEOs, and politicians. Patients were flying from all across the country to see him. It was his kingdom, and he seemed to view everyone as his minions. No one was exempt from his authoritarian approach. Our relationship was volatile. I don't like to be controlled or disrespected, so it was oil and water from the start.

When I started in the Practice one year before Dr. Weber arrived, I was the only urologist. The previous urologists had left because of illness and relocation. As the lone surgeon in the

Practice, I started the work of rebuilding the operations and services. The administration's goal was to hire a very visible and well-known "star" urologist as chief to compete in the newly emerging and profitable subspecialty of robotic surgery. Even as I focused on providing outstanding care, it was lonely being the only doctor in the office. Our training is very collaborative, with teams rounding, discussing patient care and the latest developments in the field, and I looked forward to a time when I would have that dynamic in the practice. Thus, when Dr. Weber was hired, I was excited.

The trumpets sounded, the bands gathered, and we all lined the parade route awaiting the "star." He didn't disappoint! Adorned in leather, he blazed in on a black Harley Davidson motorbike, and my world turned upside down. It seemed as if he considered my contributions to be of little value. As women in surgery, there is a tendency to minimize our value and worth, underpay us for the same level of work as our male colleagues, and pass us over for promotion. So his attitude did not come as a surprise.

Dr. Weber came to herald the division into the spotlight, and it was all about him. His leadership style was authoritarian, and there was no collaboration. Even more disconcerting was that he seemed to have no emotional IQ and would explode if I did not march to the beat of his drum. Many of his interactions were accompanied by insulting and demeaning statements, and because this was not isolated to me, I tried not to take things personally. No one ever checked his behavior. As the star surgeon, these behaviors are often accepted as par for the course. Whenever Dr. Weber opened his mouth, everyone jumped to attention, except me. That drove him crazy and fanned the flames. This took a toll on me. Every time I saw him, my heart rate quickened, and my blood pressure rose as I braced for a negative interaction. If I caught myself in time, I would mentally put up my "Not today" block, but sometimes things happened too quickly.

We were on opposite sides of the spectrum. In the present-day reality of medicine, finding the intersection between patient and profit, care and cash, character and capitulation, calling and contract, can be very challenging as many of us were not trained with a business lens. When the lens is solely business, it can lead to clinical choices that are sometimes unethical and illegal. As talented as he was, I had little respect for my chief. My friends would ask me why I was still there. Why, *was* I still there? The hospital was fifteen minutes from my home and five minutes from my son's school. My husband worked there. I loved the nurses and the OR staff, and gosh darn it, I was there first!

I was a firsthand witness to the double standards—the practices and behaviors that I believed administrators turned a blind eye to because he was the star—and this was upsetting. He called me the "angry Black woman" to use the stereotype to diminish me. Was I? I was annoyed and disgusted, but angry? No. Anger suggests an irrational and uncontrolled emotion, and I was not that. The descriptor transferred the issue from him to me. It shifted where the focus needed to lay so that instead of addressing his behavior, he created the all-too-common smokescreen of the Black woman label.

I bumped into him one day, waiting for the elevator, and he said in his heavy German accent, "Oneeka, why you look mad when you see me?"

"Do you mean why I don't giggle and bat my eyes whenever I see you?" I responded.

Honestly, I don't think a week went by without him trying to bulldoze me about something. He had just unilaterally decided that my administrative assistant would cover for his executive assistant, who had given less than 24-hour notice she was taking the following day off. I had selected my assistant from a pool of candidates to manage my practice needs and travel with me to my busy off-site clinics. As far as he was concerned, his needs superseded everyone else's, and as a result, my clinic was short-changed so that they could fully staff his clinic. The thing that would drive him crazy was that I would challenge him whenever he breached my boundaries, and then he would act confused about why I was annoyed. His response in that situation was that he was the chief, and my assistant didn't work for me; she worked for him. He wanted to have carte blanche over everything in the environment. I had to make a choice. I could allow the stress to continue to weather my physiology and lead to early death, or I could reach down and find unlimited grace to protect me from internalizing the toxicity.

One morning, I entered the conference room for our departmental meeting, and he barked, "You're late!"

Excuse me, I thought. Imagine, I had worked with our manager to schedule the staff meeting because we had not had one in over a year despite it being his responsibility as division chief to convene regular meetings. Thus, I had done his job by initiating the meeting that he was supposed to lead!

Pssssst! Lean in. Can I share a secret with you? I have a complicated relationship with time! I always try to squeeze thirty-six hours into twenty-four hours! I'm a work in progress! Despite the strategy of setting my clock fifteen minutes ahead, it seems as if I am always running five minutes behind. It drives me crazy, but I have learned to extend myself grace, and I am getting better.

It is not surprising that my German, Arnold Schwarzenegger-type division chief, a stickler for time, would be irritated. It didn't matter whether we were in a room of 10 people or 100 people; he would constantly interrupt the proceedings to call me out. I also knew that his wrath was not isolated to me, but in those moments when I was the recipient, it felt as if I was on a ledge by myself.

His attempt to criticize me that morning took me back to 11-year-old me. I was sitting on the stage during play practice, and my English teacher broadcast that she could see my underwear. Presumably, she wanted me to shift positions, but I promptly responded that my underwear was clean, which generated immediate detention and a call to my mother! Well, that impertinent 11-year-old rose that morning with my division chief, and I put my hand up and declared "Not today" to being diminished.

I said coldly, "I hope you understand by now some things will never change."

You could have heard a pin drop in the conference room. The eyes in the room shifted in slow motion from me to him.

Oh crap! Beads of perspiration sprung out on my upper lip! It was as if I had thrown a match on a pile of fireworks soaked in gasoline. Dr. Weber's face turned beet red, his mouth twisted in a snarl, and he exploded. He ranted, raged, and yelled that I was the one who convened the meeting, and now I was late and disrespectful of everyone's time. Remember, I convened the meeting that was his responsibility to assist because he had neglected that aspect of his chief role. I could feel the blistering sting of the tongue-lashing on my back. I was hurt and humiliated, but I refused to buckle. For nine years, this guy had tried to hijack my joy. Holding back my tears, I raised my head in defiance and looked at him with disdain. That further infuriated him. I stood like David facing Goliath, wishing that I had a slingshot and pondering that if I had to take him down, I was targeting urology territory and aiming for the crown jewels! I held my tongue and sat down. Lord, give me grace!

In that moment of crushing verbal abuse, I put my hand up and said, "Not today, bully. I will not do this today." This guy had no power over me. My Habits of Positivity rose in my spirit, and I placed them in my Life Slingshot with a singular purpose. Like the five stones in David's slingshot, I launched the habits one at a time. He was the epitome of a bully, and I would not allow him to prevent me from connecting to my joy and the purpose for which I was called to medicine. He would not win.

During his rant, it was as if I developed X-ray vision. I saw beyond the heart that was cold, rigid, and so encased in robotic steel that it was hidden from the light. I saw that his value lived in his ability to control others. He was mad as heck that I was not yielding to his will. To survive in the toxic environment, I had closed my heart to him, and it was killing me on the inside because that was just not me. As I watched him rant, it was almost as if I had an out-of-body experience.

As crazy as it sounds, I felt sorry for him. I decided to walk in my divine positivity super power. I could deploy my slingshot and clock him right between the eyes. For the first time, I recognized what he had seen all along, which was that I had the power of a love and grace that he did not know or understand, nor could he control. It was as if he was living in darkness, and I was a bright light that caused such pain in his eyes that he was forced to squint. That others were drawn to my light competed with his need to dominate everything in his path, and he was intent on extinguishing the light so that he could be comfortable. He also didn't know my *HOP #4*: I lived out my unique divine purpose in every moment.

Nothing is accidental. I started playing gospel music, praying, and scattering my positivity dust everywhere. I took control of how I perceived the environment. I decided I would not allow who he was to control who I was, and that started by extending grace, the same undeserving grace that God extends to me.

Extending grace does not mean you have no boundaries. It is a mindset that helps you to understand the incredible nature of your internal "God in you" S.U.P.E.R. powers.

Sometimes we think extending grace is about the other person, but it often brings us into contact with our remarkable powers. I started being cordial to him and even smiling. When he tried to be controlling, I would conjure up an image of my Life Slingshot, take deep breaths, and visualize slaying him with the Habits of Positivity, one habit at a time. My heart rate and blood pressure would remain stable, and I would calmly respond or communicate my concerns. I could separate his issues from mine, own mine, and return his to him.

Caring for Others

A few years later, it seemed as if Dr. Weber's world unraveled gradually. His personal life fell apart—he went through a divorce, and his mother died. He made some clinical choices that would come back to haunt him. Even though he pushed through with surgeries to make his numbers, he seemed tired and burned out. He was even late for conferences and eventually stopped showing up at all. He appeared to be preoccupied and just going through the motions.

Even though he was the chief, I was the leader. How many of you find yourself doing the work of the chief without the title and compensation? That was me. The staff came to me with issues and problems that needed to be resolved. As much as I tried to avoid adding anything else to my plate, it became clear that I would need to be more active in the clinic's operations. I remember the day I entered Dr. Weber's office and told him my plan to step into this role. It was pretty bold as I did not ask for permission. He blew a gasket! However, I had come prepared with my Life Slingshot loaded up with the Habits of Positivity. I spoke to him calmly and with empathy while extending grace. I acknowledged how tough things must be for him and communicated that I understood how much of an emotional struggle he was in. I gently but firmly explained that while he was dealing with his difficulties, it would create stability for the staff and fewer distractions for him if I took over the clinical operations. The *Habits* hit him right between his eyes, and the impact stunned him! I don't know if anyone had ever spoken to him in that way. I was walking in my purpose of caring for others, and our mission as a division was bigger than any one person.

"Can you tell me your ideas?" he asked.

I laid out my culture of C's for the division. I designated the Division as a "No Confusion Zone." We will focus on caring, competence, community, collaboration, cordiality, confidentiality, and accountability.

"How did you learn this?" he asked.

"I've learned people," I responded. "When we treat people like they are valued, they usually show up ready to be valuable."

"May I ask you a personal question?" he asked me. "I'm having a problem with my girlfriend...."

What the *##¥£#?! "Excuse me?" I stuttered.

Dr. Weber wanted my advice on how to handle a situation where he and his girlfriend had a difference of opinion. My archenemy then poured out his soul to me. That started almost daily conversations between us, which felt so out of this world, given where we had started. An act of compassion and grace had opened a part of this person they did not know existed. How often are you in situations where you are engaged with someone who seems to be such an overwhelming personality on the outside, and you discover it was just a cover? A cover for insecurity. A cover for trauma. A cover for fear. A cover for self-doubt. A cover for not feeling worthy of being loved. A cover for a big gaping hole on the inside that they do not know how to fill. I then understood why I was much more of a threat to my chief than I realized. I amplified all the feelings of inadequacy that were in hiding.

I saw Dr. Weber's eyes open more and more. Instead of closing them to my light, he allowed himself to adjust. Then came the questions similar to those he first asked me when I presented my office plan.

"How do you stay so positive? How do you seem to have so much joy? How are you able to be so content? Why is everyone always so drawn to you? How did you become so wise?" he would ask.

"I just want to find peace," he would say.

In our exchanges, I understood he was seeing the "God in me," but he could not see it in himself because he did not believe in God. Somehow, his childhood experiences had led him to believe that he had to control his destiny. It was the key to his survival, and that was the approach that had propelled him to his success. I simply shared with him where my peace, strength, confidence, and grace came from, and I could see the wheels turning as he asked for more and more of those stories from the Bible that seemed to mirror what he was experiencing. He really related to scripture on Job!

I was like a broken record whenever he spoke of his quest for peace and unconditional love. I would respond that there was only one place to find that peace and unconditional love, and that was with God. He laughed it off until the Patriots were down 25 to 3 in the final minutes of the 2017 Super Bowl game against the Falcons. Weber looked heavenward and said, "Whoever you are up there, please do something." As if in a flash, the Patriots scored repeatedly and won the Super Bowl 34-28. He came looking for me the next day to share that breakthrough, as he was incredulous that in that moment of desperation, he had switched into a "by any means necessary" mode. He had tested this notion of a God and was astounded how quickly God had responded to his prayer! Even though he remained skeptical, it intrigued him that he always felt encouraged and hopeful after our chats.

To say that this turn of events fascinated me would be a gross understatement. I had the most challenging time reconciling this new vulnerable and broken person in front of me, for whom I now felt compassion—and to whom I was extending a ton of grace —with the tyrant and bully that I had grown accustomed to dueling. Sometimes I would have to pinch myself because it was as if I were in the twilight zone. We developed an unlikely friendship, and at some of his lowest moments, I would hug him the same way I hugged my patients and friends. However, I had to establish boundaries and regulate his access to my time because I am a fixer by nature. I was not a therapist, and he needed one badly. Interestingly, there was humility creeping into his interactions. He was just as astounded as I that he had laid himself bare before me and sought out my insights frequently. Within the office environment, he would apologize, at least after he had flown off the handle and took more time to express appreciation to the staff and tried to remember their names. This could only be God, and I believed that this was a part of my assignment. HOP #4: I was living out my unique divine purpose in every moment, and it was linked to caring for others.

A Higher Power and Divine Purpose

In our Caribbean culture, it is much more likely for the girls to be socialized into caretaking roles, and it is not surprising that carried over into my choice to go into medicine. Given the opportunity, I would care for the entire world at my expense. This experience challenged me to set up some boundaries. I checked myself to make sure that I was not becoming some type of unhealthy crutch. I developed discernment to understand what was mine to fix. Even though my first Habit of Positivity is there is always a solution, I understand I don't always have to *be* the solution!

My chief's picture of success was to have a wife, 2.5 children, a dog, a white picket fence, and a career that made lots of money. As his personal life was disintegrating, he was desperate to reconstruct it. As his new relationships crumbled, so too did his emotional state. One day he was so distraught and desperate that he called to ask if he could accompany me to church.

Well, I'll be darned! I thought.

"Don't expect me to convert," he said. "I'm just coming to see what this is all about."

"Of course!" I replied. "I have no expectations."

I believe we don't walk this life alone, and recognizing the existence of a higher power—a power outside of ourselves that is benevolent, loves us, and wants the best for us—is germane to our well-being and peace. There is liberation in knowing that we don't always have to figure out everything ourselves. For me, that higher power is God, and I could tell that my chief was curious because what he had been doing was not working for him. It was as if he were in freefall, and he clutched for my hand to help stem the descent. As unbelievable as it may sound, I held his hand with one of mine and God's hand with the other, extended *grace*, and released my slingshot with *HOP #4*—I was living out my unique divine purpose in every moment.

It was a part of my assignment. How did I know this? All of it made such little sense that I knew there could only be one author behind the script.

That Sunday, we must have looked like Mutt and Jeff. Dr. Weber was dressed in a confident GQ way. His rugged good looks, blond, spiked hair, and towering six-foot five-inch well-built frame that dwarfed me made him stand out. He looked like a fish out of water in our predominantly Black church. The young people performed a reggae gospel jam, and he moved awkwardly but with great appreciation to the Jamaican vibes. Our Bishop preached, "You are God's masterpiece." It was as if Dr. Weber had never been in a space where he had heard of his worth, which was not dependent on who he was but *whose* he was, and that the sacrifice had already been made for him to always have access. At the beginning of the service, I could feel the tension radiating from him like heat from a pile of red-hot coal. Gradually, I saw a relaxation of his shoulders as he gave himself permission to release all preconceived notions and assume a posture to receive God's love. For the first time, I could sense a calming of his soul and peace in his spirit. When Bishop Greene asked who wanted to know this Jesus who loved us unconditionally and died for the forgiveness of all our sins, a shock of all shockers, my archenemy raised his hand. With tears in his eyes, he told me after the service, "I am God's masterpiece."

I had loaded up my Life Slingshot, launched my Habits of Positivity, and extended grace and compassion. Given the years of downright abuse that I had endured, it would have been reasonable to stay angry and revel in his downfall. Instead, I held my hand up and said "Not today" to revenge and gloating and instead said yes to kindness and compassion. I got to connect to and actualize the God power within me, and on that Sunday, Dr. Weber made a decision that gave him access to heaven—maybe that was the purpose for which I was planted in that division of urology.

Even as Dr. Weber and I developed a more amicable relationship, there was still an underlying systemic dysfunction that had chipped away at me over time. I needed to take a break. I decided to take a year-long sabbatical beginning that June. Coincidentally, several poor decisions came home to roost for Dr. Weber, and he took a leave of absence at the same time. We kept in touch intermittently, and I could tell he was struggling.

The persistent ringing of my phone jarred me out of a deep sleep one Monday morning in May. *What the heck,* I thought, as I fumbled to find the phone in the dark. Phone calls at that hour are never good, and as I looked at the caller ID and saw my office manager's number, I had a deep sense of foreboding.

I answered the phone, my heart in my hands and voice trembling, as I asked, "What's wrong, Connie?" She was crying hysterically.

"Dr. Weber killed his wife," she said. "I just can't believe this... I just can't believe this," she kept repeating. "It is all over the news," she said as she described what she had heard.

My heart threatened to jump out of my chest, and my mind was numb with shock. I was overcome by waves of extreme sadness. This was tragic. Sometimes I wondered if Dr. Weber would take his own life but I never imagined this scenario where his downward spiral would take this turn.

I was in a vortex of emotions ranging from disbelief to anger to grief to intense sadness to compassion to confusion to guilt. The fixer in me asked whether there was something I could have done? I could not stop thinking about his wife, their children, and I could not stop thinking about him. I tried to wipe him out of my mind. I had come to know a different version of my chief and felt like I had dug below the robot's surface to expose his humanity. I discovered a product of childhood trauma, a casualty of physician burnout —unrecognized and unaddressed—and over time, the dominoes fell one after the other in quick succession. I wrestled with feeling devastated for his wife and children while feeling so sad for him. I read articles that described the ongoing abuse that his wife had reported, and my heart bled that she had endured such suffering at his hands. This increased my resolve to put that chapter of my life behind me.

Then, months later, out of the blue, I received word that Dr. Weber asked whether I might visit him in prison. *No way, I don't want to get sucked back in. I could not imagine how I could sit with him knowing that, after killing his wife, he had put rocks in her pockets and thrown her in a pond. I couldn't do it.* Yet, somehow, it felt as if I was being sent on a final mission of grace, and it seemed like the hand of God. *Really God? That's crazy!* I prayed and prayed and prayed, and I kept hearing the same response: His grace is sufficient. It's not my grace, but God's unlimited grace.

As I drove up to the barbed-wire prison compound, my apprehension threatened to defeat my courage. *Was I doing the right thing?* Even scheduling the visit was daunting: Fill out a form online with a lot of personal information; wait nervously for approval, a part of me hoping that I would be denied, and the decision would have been made for me. Approval was granted, and I called the prison repeatedly until someone answered the phone. As his name haltingly rolled off my tongue, the horror of the reality sliced me to the core as I registered to be his one visitor that week. The day was as gloomy as I felt. Dark gray clouds painted the sky, the constant drizzle of cold rain punctuating my damp mood, and the tall, gray fences surrounding the prison discouraged my approach.

I had never entered a prison before, and I gazed curiously but surreptitiously at the other visitors, wondering what their stories were. Who were they visiting, and how were they feeling? Some had an air of familiarity as they went through the check-in process, and a few others had the same hesitant vibe as I did, marking them as first-timers. As I completed the COVID-19 screening and paperwork, I paused at the section that asked for my relationship with the inmate. Was I a friend? Was I just a colleague? I ended up writing down both, feeling that I could not deny that we had brokered a fragile friendship. Feeling as if I was starring in a scene from a dystopian movie, I stripped off all jewelry and placed my belongings in a small locker before going through metal detectors and three locked doors.

Finally, I entered a room that looked like everything I had ever seen in the movies. Floor-to-ceiling plexiglass separated visitors from the inmates. The visitor area was divided into cubicles, with wall phones on either side of the plexiglass. I waited with four other visitors as the gate clanked and the inmates marched into the other half of the room. As I watched Dr. Weber approach, outfitted in an orange jumpsuit, hair in a buzz cut, looking considerably thinner than the last time I saw him, I grieved the loss of a mother, daughter, sister, and friend and truthfully, I could not help but mourn the loss of a father, brother, and surgeon. I felt bereft.

The entire experience was surreal. Was I really visiting the former chief of urology, the "star" of our urology division, in prison? *Was I stupid to come?* He put his hand up to the glass in greeting, and I placed my hand on the glass and looked into his eyes, searching for elusive answers. I stumbled through the maze of memories falling over the image of him always operating on the robot barefoot. Somehow that reminded me of the hours upon hours of skin-to-skin time that I did with our premature son Mark, building that intimate connection where we moved as one. That's how it was with the chief and his robot. Was he walking barefoot in his cell?

I tripped over the memory of Karen, his wife, who was so excited that I was going to include a robot character with a heart of steel, modeled after her husband, in my children's books. He asked me one day if Rolf the Robot's heart would ever warm up. His question introduced a twist that I had not considered. He acknowledged he had felt a shift in his heart and was looking for affirmation that I felt the shift as well. As I came back to the present, I saw in his eyes an impaired physician, a burned-out physician, a runaway train that careened unchecked and crashed with a horrendous explosion that destroyed lives around it. It didn't have to be this way. Sadly, so many physicians crash and burn, and that epidemic has gotten worse during COVID. Even though he had committed an unbelievably heinous act and had been such a beast to me for so many years, I felt compassion for him. His eyes shone with gratitude at my gesture of being open to connection by placing my hands against his on the plexiglass. I wondered if I would somehow wake up from this nightmare. I imagine he felt the same way. Weber signaled that he needed to enter a code into the phone on his side, and my heart broke as he entered the numbers automatically—now seared into his life code, forever altered.

The star surgeon had been reduced to a shell of shame and regret but recalled how encouraged he had felt during our many office conversations. And instantly, I knew why God had sent me here. To deliver the reminder that he was still God's masterpiece and that there was nowhere he could go where he was beyond God's reach. I marveled that the first resource he had reached out to in prison was the chaplain, as he yearned to develop the type of faith that I had often spoken of. He shared that he had nothing else to hold onto as he had lost everything. I ministered that even as he paid for the consequences of his actions, God could still use him. His expertise and knowledge could allow him to serve the men with whom he came into contact. I would never have imagined that my assignment would be about his redemption and salvation when he came striding into my world twelve years prior. I had picked up my slingshot one more time, and now my assignment was complete. God's grace is sufficient.

I learned a lot about toxic relationships during my tenure in that practice. How many of you have found yourself in friendships or work situations that are toxic and unhealthy? Many of us remain in situations where we become comfortable with the discomfort because the thought of change is more daunting. We become hotter and hotter, sweating bullets while putting out little fires left and right but don't shift until the whole house burns down. These situations create physical wear and tear that many times go unrecognized. If you are in tune with your body, you may feel the rise of your blood pressure or shallowness of your breath while in the presence of a toxic person or situation. That physical response of constant fight-or-flight keeps your system on high alert and "weathers" your body. I had to learn to use the Habits of Positivity to protect myself.

I considered toxicity to be like inclement weather. Whether one is experiencing slight drizzles (micro-aggressions) or downpours (macro-aggressions), or hurricanes (toxic relationships), there are some protections we can deploy. We can put up our umbrellas, don our raincoats, or remove ourselves from the storm by taking cover. The Habits of Positivity are like umbrellas and raincoats. They require us to have a measure of awareness to be intentional about utilizing our protective gear. Sometimes there is an assignment during the storm, but there comes the point when you have to remove yourself from toxic environments or people. Though my relationship had improved with my chief, the environment that had supported his toxicity had not changed, and I knew I had to remove myself from the storm. For that reason, I took a break. Toxic or traumatic experiences demand that we must take time to heal from the bumps, bruises, and wounds. I took my power back in the relationship with my chief by using my positivity habits and certainly experienced post-traumatic growth. It was also important for me to recognize the experiences as trauma and be intentional about creating time and space for self-care and healing.

UROLOGY STORY:
EXTENDING GRACE TO MY PATIENTS—
AND MYSELF

Now and again, there will be an alienating interaction with a patient, and you have to remind yourself of your divine assignment. As a woman in surgery, this can occur in a few ways, but most commonly, it manifests in the assumption that you are everything else but the surgeon. These episodes occur even more frequently as a Black female surgeon. For many years I would take umbrage at being mistaken for the dietary staff, the medical secretary, or the medical assistant. There is nothing wrong with any of these pursuits, but why did the reverse assumption never occur? Sadly, I understood that if one looked at the statistics, those patients' assessments were absolutely correct. I did not look like a typical urologic surgeon. So instead of being offended, I extended grace, took out my slingshot, and fully embraced that part of my purpose is to expose patients to the notion that a urologic surgeon could look like me. The excellence that I bring to caring for them will change their perception and worldview forever.

I knew that being a urologist was part of my life's calling, and I remember the moment that was revealed to me. In a similar vein, I can recall the first moment when I questioned that decision! During my first month in practice after completing residency, I strode confidently into the exam room to be greeted by a plump, middle-aged man. I could tell he was nervous. His dewy face had a peaked look. His pale blue eyes shifted everywhere except to connect with mine, and his cold, clammy handshake was a definite tip-off. His eyes darted past me as I introduced myself, almost as if he thought there had been a mistake. Indeed, I could not possibly be the doctor.

I sat on the exam stool, moving in closer, straining to hear, as he haltingly described the two years of frustration related to recurrent infections of his penile foreskin. His embarrassment was palpable, so we chatted lightly about less sensitive matters, and his voice became more audible as he relaxed. He became too relaxed! As we transitioned to me examining his genitals, I needed to manipulate the foreskin to assess scarring. Suddenly, I sensed a jerking motion of his body. I felt as if I turned my head in slow motion to look at his face, and his eyes were rolled back in his head. *Holy Moly! Is he having a seizure? Goodness gracious, this can't be happening!* I didn't even know if we had a medical emergency code cart. A million thoughts were racing through my head. *Remember ACLS training—A, B, C: Airway, Breathing, Circulation.*

A warm sensation on my hands yanked me back to the present. A volcanic eruption of white viscous fluid was flowing into my gloves. I was in a fog, my brain refusing to register what had just happened. Was that semen all over my gloves? The startling reality was that he had just ejaculated, and I thought, *What the heck was I thinking being a urologist?*

I took a deep breath and mustered the courage not to flee the room. I looked up at him. Lord have mercy. His eyes were closed. The look of post-ejaculatory bliss, a mixture of peace and euphoria, was plastered on his face. Nothing in my training had prepared me for this. The feelings crashed on me at warp speed: disbelief, revulsion, confusion, embarrassment, fear. I felt disrespected and cheapened and just wanted to escape that room. Then, I was annoyed, and thoughts raced through my mind on how to bring him painfully crashing down to Earth. I resisted. Instead, I remained as cool as a cucumber on the outside, completed the exam, took off my gloves, and advised him I would leave the room so he could get cleaned up and dressed.

I was shaking as soon as I exited the room and did not know how to go back in. I had to shoehorn myself into a place of grace. I wasn't feeling charitable, but I had to consider the notion that maybe he also felt badly. Maybe he was embarrassed. When I re-entered the room, he did not apologize or acknowledge what had happened. Yet again, I extended grace that maybe he had yet another urologic problem that needed to be addressed—premature ejaculation! However, I no longer felt comfortable caring for him. I was conflicted because our mission as doctors is accounted for in HOP #4, which is caring for others, so I wrestled with what to do. I extended grace to myself and acknowledged that it was okay to set boundaries. Sometimes you can point others in the solution's direction, but you don't have to *be* the solution. That's what I did with this patient. I transferred his care to one of my male partners, thus ensuring that he received the care he needed. Caring for others does not mean that we have to sacrifice ourselves. There is harmony between the two because you cannot possibly effectively care for others in a sustained way if you don't care for yourself. That interaction did not steer me away from my purpose, and I did not allow that negative encounter to cause me to discontinue seeing male patients. I used my Habits of Positivity to place the experience in context, and you can too.

How often do you find yourself in situations that make no sense? Meaning, situations that are so irritating that it feels as if there is sand in your eyes? How do you respond? Do you scratch your eyes out, causing even more discomfort? Do you close your eyes and ignore the sensation rather than examine how the sand got into your eyes? How many times have you looked back at an uncomfortable situation but, in retrospect, understood that you were placed in that situation to grow and learn so that you can use your story to have an impact that only you can have? How do you think about yourself at those times? Do you embrace the opportunity to launch your slingshot, or do you develop imposter syndrome? Do you compare everyone else's slingshot to yours and feel a sense of lack that all you have is a rudimentary slingshot? When you experience that limiting self-talk, remember David and Goliath. A simple slingshot defeated an army. It was about the slingshot, what David put in it and what he believed. Pick up your Life Slingshot, put your *Habits of Positivity* in it, and believe that His grace is sufficient for you to launch!

POSITIVITY PAUSE

How can you use your Life Slingshot to deliver unlimited grace? How can you not allow circumstances to defeat you and prevent toxic personalities from blocking your joy? Unleash your S.U.P.E.R. powers of positivity and fire unlimited grace to defeat the limited thinking monster that drives toxic behaviors. Your Life Slingshot is a perfect way to launch a counterattack. Keep loading it until you hit the mark. It may not happen the first time as it will require practice, so don't give up.

Slingshots first pull backward before advancing. Growth and power build in the tension of the bands. The maximal stretch point is where the most power is harnessed, so when it feels as if you are at your limit, know that the potential energy stored in that stretch will change lives.

Sometimes you will overstretch, and the slingshot band will break. It's not the end of the world. The road to success will be paved with failures. Take stock and try again!

Identify your target because you have an impact and purpose.

We all have Life Slingshots. It doesn't matter if the material, color, or projectiles are different. We have a common purpose: to make a difference in someone's life.

What do I put in my slingshot? I put the 5 Habits of Positivity!

1. There is always a solution; work to find it.

2. Convert a limit into an opportunity.

3. Keep the positive; discard the negative.

4. You are unique, with a divine purpose linked to caring for others.

5. Be thankful and believe.

I encourage you to put those habits in your slingshot too, along with your skills and talents but also load your slingshot with love, understanding, generosity, kindness, joy, compassion, tolerance, forgiveness, gentleness, inclusiveness, hope, sensitivity, respect, courage, resilience, optimism, mercy, grace, purpose, and justice.

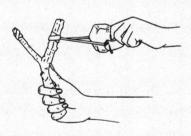

POSITIVITY PRACTICE

Release Your Life Slingshot

1. Meditate on what your slingshot looks like.

2. What did you put in your slingshot today?

3. Reflect on experiences where you felt the stretch of your slingshot being pulled back.

4. Reflect on experiences where you aimed, released, and hit the target using grace.

5. Sit for 10 minutes every day and list when you placed the Habits of Positivity in your Life Slingshot and the impact that resulted.

TRANSFORMATION

Reflect on the differences between when you did not load your Life Slingshot with grace or the Habits of Positivity versus how you feel now that you are using your Life Slingshot. Journal your responses below:

Before I started using my Life Slingshot to understand that there will be times when life will pull me back, but I can load up my Habits of Positivity, I used to feel:

Now that I use my Life Slingshot daily and understand that being pulled backward allows me to actively load, aim, and release my Habits of Positivity, I feel:

Unlimited Power— Positivity Champion

"My strength and power are made perfect and show themselves effective in your weakness."

—2 CORINTHIANS 12:9

> *"What I want young women and girls to know is: You are powerful and your voice matters."*
>
> **—KAMALA HARRIS**

HOW MANY OF YOU HAVE read the *Harry Potter* books or seen the movies? Do you remember Harry's Patronus—the white stag that he could call forth whenever he needed extreme protection? That was his Positivity Champion. You, too, have a Positivity Champion—an awakened secret self that lies dormant until needed and is then brought to light. Every Positivity Champion is unique and is comprised exclusively of positive emotions.

Do you know that each of you has a Power of Positivity that you can call forth? This is one of your internal S.U.P.E.R. powers. This harnessed positive energy will allow you to put your hand up and declare "Not today" to negativity and limited thinking. The earlier we learn to harness and launch this unlimited power, the more quickly we can transform our thinking and cope, hope, and be well during challenging times.

The Angel Who Protected Our Family

I understand that my Positivity Champion has been building since 1975. I was nine years old, living in Georgetown, Guyana, in a house elevated on concrete posts to protect us from regular floods. Mangoes were in season, the trees laden with golden orange globes of delight. The sun filtered through the stately coconut fronds, which seemed to bow to grant access to the fiery rays. Rivulets of sweat were coursing down our faces, but that did not stop my brother and me from frolicking with the neighborhood kids as we created toys from whatever castoffs we could find.

The toy of the day was my great uncle's giant rusty old bike called a "Preggie" because the slanted support bar had a big, curved belly. We wedged our legs between the bar and the belly. We rode sideways, riding as long as we could before falling off and doubling over with laughter. Our merriment would continue all day long, infecting passersby as they strolled on the sidewalk in front of the house. I also loved watching those passersby and sometimes played "hide and seek" from our front veranda porch. Workers rode back and forth on their bicycles, transporting a passenger sitting on the high crossbar that we couldn't quite straddle. The pungent scent of fresh horse manure would overwhelm my nose as the animals lumbered down the steamy asphalt streets, pulling an assortment of cargo and dumping their internal loads.

Then I saw her coming. I scampered up to the veranda, my eyes fixed on her. A delicate-faced older white woman with sparkling eyes, gray hair to her shoulders, and kind lines around her mouth walking at the same brisk pace that marked her daily passage in front of our house. She reminded me of a thinner version of my Granny Doris, who was part Portuguese with light skin and fine, straight hair that she wore in a single braid pinned up at the back of her head.

One hot, humid Georgetown afternoon, the Granny lookalike stopped at our gate and spoke to my very protective mother. Her name was Miss Medina. Even though my mom did not know her, she allowed me to attend weekly Catholic prayer meetings with this kind older woman. This continued for a year and a half until we moved from Guyana to Barbados. I remember entering the cozy living room of the prayer host, the fragrance of Yardley's powder dancing in the air, and I would burrow into soft, welcoming sofas that invited me into this safe space. I don't remember being in the least bit phased that I was the only child and Brown person in the room. I recently asked my mom why she allowed me to go to the prayer meetings with a stranger, as it was a drastic departure from her norm. She replied in a hushed tone as if now connecting to the insanity of her decision.

"When Miss Medina stopped at our gate, she told me you were special, and she saw God's light shining through you. She wanted to take you with her to prayer meetings. Somehow I knew this was out of my control, and incomprehensibly I said yes."

Six months after I began attending prayer meetings with Ms. Medina, a White man in a dark suit with slicked-down jet-black hair, state-trooper dark glasses, and an American accent knocked on our front door. He was our new neighbor and immediately gravitated to my dad's worldliness and knowledge. My dad is an accomplished journalist and was the *Reuters News Agency* correspondent in Guyana. He is practical, worldly, a critical thinker, rational, objective, and not prone to overly emotional responses. They engaged for hours on topics ranging from local politics to international affairs. The neighbor's access to the outside world was via the never-ending flow of information spilling out from my dad's Reuter's news transmitter, and so he and his team-members became a frequent visitor.

My brother and I would watch through the wooden fences in wide-eyed nine-year-old fascination as people went back and forth, speaking in a twang that we had only ever heard in the movies. We'd place bets on whether the neighbor would take off his dark glasses. Then, a year later, the dark, slick-haired man finally took off his glasses, only for a moment.

Dad recollects, "He took off his dark glasses and said, "Look into my eyes." His eyes snatched me into a dark world of strange figures, snakes and a fiery pit and I felt a force pulling my mind. I felt cold and struggled to break eye contact. Somehow I wrenched free."

Jim Jones of the People's Temple slipped his glasses over his bloodshot eyes and laughed. "You are strong, Hubert," he said to my dad. "You are very strong."

For almost three years, we lived next to the mastermind of the world's largest mass suicide, which occurred in Guyana on November 18th, 1978. Jim Jones and his followers had moved their church to Guyana between 1974-1977, with their main campus in a rural part of the country and their headquarters in the capital, Georgetown, next door to our home. For us, as children, they were a welcome distraction and added interest and intrigue to our world. For my Dad, they represented a dark presence.

What protected my dad and our family the day that Jim Jones took off his glasses? I believe God sent an angel in the form of Miss Medina. As I went to prayer meetings with Miss Medina, starting six months before Jim Jones moved in next door, there was powerful protection being called forth in that circle of prayer. At every meeting, I would recite "Hail Mary, full of grace, the Lord is with thee. Blessed art thou amongst women and blessed is the fruit of thy womb, Jesus. Holy Mary, Mother of God, pray for us sinners, now and at the hour of our death, Amen," over and over again, as my fingers marched over the pink rosary beads that Miss Medina gave me and which I still have, 44 years later. As we prayed, the source of the light that Miss Medina saw in me expanded to protect my family. This has been the light that shines forth as I walk in my purpose of championing positivity in education and health.

Jim Jones and the People's Temple became our neighbors the same year that Miss Medina saw my light, stopped, spoke to my mom, and started taking me to prayer meetings. Was that coincidence? I don't believe it was. It was divine protection and the beginnings of my Positivity Champion. Miss Medina had been my Positivity Champion and gave me what I needed to cultivate my own.

UROLOGY STORY:
LAUNCHING MY POSITIVITY CHAMPION
FOR OTHERS

I have always been a champion for the underdog. When my mom called me the "people's representative," she could have instead said Positivity Champion! If you needed protection, I was your person. So, it is not surprising that I would eventually have a practice with many patients who could not speak up for themselves. I became the urologist for many patients with varying degrees of mental retardation, autism, and psychiatric disorders. Whatever their issues, we greeted our patients cheerfully and cared for them with enthusiasm. I modeled and emphasized to my team that we were privileged to take care of all of our patients, and we lived out a part of our purpose in how we cared for and interacted with them. Our mission was to launch our Positivity Champions to help them since they could not do it for themselves.

Billy was one of those patients. He was a Down's Syndrome male in his sixties, who I had seen for over ten years because he wasn't emptying his bladder. Eventually, I had to operate on him to insert a suprapubic catheter. Billy had moderately severe mental retardation and loved football. Even though he yelled and screamed whenever I changed his catheter, he would always give me a big smile when I entered the room and say, "Hi, Doctor Wiggles!" I would ask him about the Patriots, and he would respond with a toothless grin, especially if they had won, and point to his blue cap with the Patriots logo emblazoned on the front. His post-catheter change treat was a happy meal from McDonalds, so he ended the visits on a high!

My medical assistant would change the catheter if I were not available. She is a statuesque, Black, full-figured woman with long magnetic lashes, an infectious smile, and cute dimples. True to form, Billy would start yelling as soon as she entered the room. She would respond, "Billy, I haven't even touched you," and he would grin mischievously. One day as my assistant entered the room to set up the catheter supplies, Billy's eyes lit up, and he said, "Hello, Chocolate Drop!" Our mouths almost hit the floor, and we both looked at Billy through a new lens. We had always referred to him as a Down's Syndrome male, but that day we recognized he was a man with Down's Syndrome.

How often do we put people in a box, based on external appearances or some other label, and so we miss the essence of who they are? We even do it to ourselves. But there is a way of engaging that can help unlock the divine uniqueness we all have rooted in positivity.

For all of his mental compromise, Billy felt the energy of our kindness, care, compassion, and positivity, which allowed him to access a part of himself that was buried by his physical and mental challenges. Billy was a gift, and it was a blessing to care for him. He lived a long life which was a feat for a man with Down's Syndrome. When he had repeated hospital admissions, we feared the end was near. And it was. When Billy died, we all cried because we knew we would miss hearing Doctor Wiggles and Chocolate Drop. He inspired us to be our best selves and launch our Positivity Champions, which blessed him and us at the same time.

As unreal as the Miss Medina story sounds, I believe it gives us a glimpse into our divine internal S.U.P.E.R. powers, representing the "God within us." There is a construct here that helps us understand that we can harness and launch our unlimited power. Sometimes, someone is positioned as a shepherd or guide to help us identify and harness those powers.

Can you think back to an incredibly challenging time when someone showed up as an angel to help you make it through? For that person, the assignment was a part of their purpose. How many times have you found yourself dealing with a trying situation, and someone calls at that moment because you crossed his or her mind? Or someone showed up with something that you needed at the exact time that you needed it? Or when you thought that there was no way out, someone delivered an encouraging word or made you laugh so that it lightened your mood long enough for you to feel hopeful? They were Positivity Champions.

When we respond to that little voice that directs us to make a call or visit someone, it is because we are being sent on an assignment. It's a part of our purpose, and we have to learn to listen. That's what my mom did with Ms. Medina. Let's look back at those experiences in our lives when we heard that little voice. Looking in the rearview mirror helps us harness and launch our positivity power because we can assess our situations from the perspective that an assignment prepared us to be the answer to someone else's prayer. So, either you are on the receiving end as part of someone else's assignment, or you are the one being given the assignment. How confidently would you approach situations if you believe you were specially chosen for an assignment that only you can do? Launch HOP #4: I am living out my unique divine purpose in every moment. You would walk with confidence, declaring, "yes, I am the only one for this assignment; just let me at 'em!" That's when you launch your Positivity Champion!

Sometimes, a particular person is chosen as your Positivity Champion before you can call forth your own. This person protects, inspires, guides, nurtures, and calls forth greatness from you. It could be a parent, a teacher, or a family friend. It may be someone that you don't know well but who comes into your life for the sole purpose of helping to nurture and shape your Positivity Champion. There is unlimited power deep within all of us. When you learn to uncover it, harness it, and then release it into the world, the transformation of your thinking opens the door for you to establish contact with your purpose. You develop a deep inner knowing that you have the Positivity Power to overcome, regardless of the circumstances. Keep your eyes peeled for your Positivity Champion, and visualize how launching your champion's power can change the lives of those around you.

POSiTiViTY PAUSE

You have a Positivity Champion! We all do. Take a minute to let this sink in. There is a positivity force inside of you that you can identify and name. That force is attached to your purpose, which resides in the present moment. Bill Keane, the famous cartoonist and author of *The Family Circus*, said, "Yesterday is history, tomorrow is a mystery, today is a gift from God, which is why we call it the present." A transformation occurs when you can assign a form to your unlimited power in the present moment. Name it. Call it out. Recognize how to harness and launch your Positivity Champion, and have it consistently deliver its impact every time. This is how you learn to HOP into your power and build your Scaffold of Positivity!

POSITIVITY PRACTICE

You can visualize a force of pure, focused energy of positivity by assigning a form to it and apply it to any difficulties and challenges you encounter.

Call Forth Your Inner Positivity Champion

1. Can you think back to a person in your life who has been your angel and helped call forth your Positivity Champion?

2. Close your eyes, breathe deeply and meditate on what your Positivity Champion looks like. Draw it on paper.

3. For every situation that threatens to introduce negative thoughts or when the "limited thinking" monster attacks, create the image of your Positivity Champion, loaded up with the 5 Habits of Positivity as your ammunition, and launch your counterattack.

4. At the end of each day, choose one situation where you launched your Positivity Champion and list how each of the habits slayed the "limited thinking" monster.

5. Keep a Positivity Champion board with stickies, drawings, or reflections of your launches.

TRANSFORMATION

Reflect on the differences between when you did not call upon your Positivity Champion versus how you feel now that you are using it. Journal your responses below:

Before I started launching my Positivity Champion to defend against negativity and limited thinking, I used to feel:

Now that I launch my Positivity Champion regularly, using my Habits of Positivity to slay negativity, I feel:

HABIT OF POSITIVITY #5

Be Thankful and Believe!

CHAPTER 10

Unlimited Favor—
Positivity Window

**". . . and His FAVOR is for a lifetime.
Weeping may tarry for a night but joy
comes with the morning."**

—PSALM 30:5

"Life is an opportunity, benefit from it. Life is beauty, admire it. Life is a dream, realize it."

—MOTHER TERESA

WHAT IS FAVOR? SIMPLY PUT, it means special blessings. Can you think of times in your life when you felt as if you had an abundance of favor? What about the times when things did not work out as you expected? Can you feel as if you still have favor even in the tough times? Can we prepare our children for a world that will not always be kind? Can we prepare them for challenges where the outcomes may not be defined as success? It depends upon the window through which you view your circumstances. You can choose to say "Not today" to negativity and limiting thoughts! You can make the Habits of Positivity the frame of your Positivity Window and gaze onto your Unlimited Sky of Favor wherever you are! It's a way of thinking that can change your world and that of your children.

When you can identify the favor in your life, you increase your gratitude and practice HOP #5. Feeling thankful for the good can change your entire perspective, enabling you to see more of the positives in your life. This shift will allow you to tap into more of your joy in your everyday life and give you added strength during challenging times.

Finding My Favor(ite): How I Met My Kindred Spirit

Have you ever met someone with whom you connect effort-lessly? As my grandmother would say, "Your spirit took to them." That's how it was with my husband, Charles. It was a hot and humid September day in Baltimore. I was rocking my new black-and-orange swimsuit, frolicking in the athletic-center pool like a sea nymph, braids streaming down my back. Confident now that I had survived freshman year at Johns Hopkins University, I wore that knowledge with an air of authority. He was a medical student at Johns Hopkins Medical School but was most known for his turntable skills! He rolled up to the undergraduate orientation pool party, looking suave and self-assured. DJ Funkmaster Charles sauntered over just to make sure that I knew who he was!

A few weeks later, we reconnected at a house party, traded values and visions, and exchanged family stories. We found a kindred spirit in each other—not to mention a growing attraction. It was on and popping! His birthday was a week later, and I surprised him with a dinner cruise on the Spirit of Baltimore. In retrospect, I don't know where I found the money to splurge, but I knew that I had met someone worth investing in. A month later, we took an evening stroll along the edge of the lake in Mondawmin Park. Couples cuddled on benches, soft music wafted out of parked cars housing lovers locked in an embrace, and the moonlight reflected off the waters casting a soft glow about Charles' face. It was a perfect setup, and he was dragging his feet! I could not stand the suspense!

In my usual direct way, I asked, "Well, aren't you going to kiss me?"

And so, the love connection began. He didn't judge me for making that bold first move and never seemed to think that I had somehow usurped his role as the man. Charles was tailor-made for me and me for Charles! Favor!

We became as inseparable as was possible, given that we were both in rigorous programs. Our nerdy dates were usually at the library, and it was as if each of our houses gained a housemate. I lived with six women, and Charles was frequently the only male at the dinner table. Charles lived with Alpha fraternity brothers, and I was often the only woman in the house. When I left for college, my parents reminded me they expected me to stay straight and narrow—focus and work hard. This really wasn't challenging. I'd been doing it all my life. What I wasn't prepared for was falling in love!

Charles was a talker, analyzing everything into the ground. I was a hard-nosed West Indian woman, not prone to being overly emotionally expressive. I kept things close to my chest. No way was I going to be vulnerable and expose my heart. I don't even think I knew how! Wooowee! You can just imagine how interesting that was! He could break through my typical silent treatment whenever I was bothered. There were days when he wore me out with his over-analyzing, and I would throw my hands up and exclaim, "Not today!" But yet he persisted! Our dance of interaction became more coordinated as we gained a deeper understanding of each other and weathered the standard young-love roller coaster.

I was content to keep him a well-hidden secret, letting my parents think I spent all of my time studying. For those of you ladies who have brothers, you can probably guess that didn't last long! My brother spilled the beans about me having a boyfriend a few months in. I knew my parents would view the relationship as a distraction, and I was determined to prove them wrong. We earned our life stripes as we managed responsibility and relationships. He visited Barbados the following Christmas and fit right into the family. Christmases in Barbados were the highlight of our year: tropical splendor, beaches, Santa on jet skis, sunrise services on Christmas morning, brand new outfits on display, and listening to the police band in Queens Park, nestled in the capital city of Bridgetown. After our sixth consecutive Christmas in Barbados, Charles' mom asked in a somewhat peeved tone why we never came to Buffalo at Christmas! As we struggled not to state the obvious, we acknowledged we wanted to be fair and not establish a competitive dynamic between the families. We agreed that my entire family would travel to Buffalo for the following Christmas. That Christmas of 1997 in Buffalo, New York, it snowed in a way that we had never experienced! Eighteen inches fell so rapidly that we could not see three feet in front of our car. However, indoors, there was a feeling of the warmth of family love, celebration, community, and fellowship. This shifted our perspective from being annoyed that we were freezing and dealing with snow instead of relaxing on the beach in 90-degree weather. We were looking through the Window of Favor and enthralled by the beauty and spectacle of the Winter Wonderland. This created the backdrop for a Christmas that we would never forget. A once-in-a-lifetime experience! However, we agreed that Christmases in Barbados should be the family tradition, and all were welcome to join us!

Favor Extended in Family-in-Law

The Andersons loved nothing better than a party, and holidays were tailor-made for them! Barbeque ribs, collard greens, potato salad, and sweet potato pie were a few of the mouth-watering treats that Charles told me to prepare for as we made the pilgrimage from Baltimore to Buffalo for the 4th of July festivities. There were butterflies in my stomach the first time we drove up to his childhood home. I didn't need to be anxious about anything. Charles' dad greeted me, beaming from ear to ear, and said, "Uhnica (he never got the O-neee-ka syllables quite right), welcome to the family, maan," in his lilting Jamaican accent!

Dr. Charles Anderson Sr. was tenacious as a young man, leaving Saint Ann's, Jamaica, in his early twenties, with just the clothes on his back and a dream of a better life in Buffalo, New York. He was a force of nature and believed that "can't" did not belong in his or his children's vocabulary. Fun-loving, an avid golfer, and a dancer, we were kindred spirits who shared a never-ending optimism that fueled big dreams. From his lowly beginnings, he opened up the first Black Family Practice medical group in Western New York and became a stalwart of community activism and advancing health in Buffalo and Jamaica. Dr. Anderson Sr. was focused on legacy before we understood the vastness of how impactful legacy is for our family and the many ways that legacy is created. All of his children bear his middle initial "L," and he wanted generations of his offspring to carry on the tradition. What's in an initial, one might ask? Imagine looking onto your sky of favor and seeing the "L" and all the rich history, affirmation, connections, love, and hope encapsulated in that single letter. Even until his death at age eight-one, he was still planning and dreaming of one big project after another. I loved chatting with him because he was enthusiastic and excited about everything I did. When he died, despite the acute pain of our loss, we could look out of our Positivity Window onto the sky of unlimited favor. We give thanks for the impact that his legacy created in our lives.

Just as incredible is Charles's mom, Queen Bea! The Queen is one of a kind! She was born in Mississippi, picking cotton as a child; she is a Pisces and a diva-like no other. She has a full-blown love affair with life and lives each day to the fullest. Every milestone is recognized and celebrated. She must have a mail fairy because, even as she attracts friends like bees to honey, every milestone or holiday is accompanied by a card or package from Queen Bea! After our son Mark was born, she came to spend more time with us in Boston, and we discovered a shared passion for creativity, cooking, style, entertaining, and shopping. Queen Bea's hat, handbag, jewelry, outfit, and shoes were always well-coordinated. It was she who kicked my style up a few notches, as I needed to represent my generation. She trained me well, and I think I have achieved my style stripes that make me eligible to be a part of her entourage! We are two peas in a pod, and it was no wonder that "my spirit took to Charles," as the old West Indians would say. It was an enormous blessing and inspiring to have parents-in-law who exuded positivity and energy despite their early hardships. Our families blended, with parents on both sides and siblings having great relationships with one another—unlimited favor.

Building Our Scaffold of Positivity Together

Charles started Princeton at fifteen and did not become a social outcast because the university incorrectly listed his age as eighteen on his university ID. He met Gary, and they formed their DJ crew. They spent countless weekends road-tripping to colleges up and down the East Coast. When we met, he had a sports car—a cute gold Mazda RX-7 with black louvers and a black canvas bra over the headlights. It was all the way tricked out! We continued the road-tripping tradition, mostly visiting my brother and best friend in Philadelphia, family in Buffalo and New York City, and the occasional DJ gig. We strategized, laughed, and enjoyed having a good time with family and friends on those long drives. We dreamed big, unlimited dreams. We fully embraced HOP #5: We were thankful for so many things, and we believed we would change the world!

Imagine cramming five people into the two-seater Mazda RX-7. We did so on a few occasions and were pulled over by the police one of those times. However, we were often pulled over just for "driving while Black," and I'd have to talk Charles down off the ledge, or he would've inevitably wound up hurt or in jail. I didn't see that side of him often, but it was usually at some profiling stop. The admixture of fear and repressed anger would strip away the dignity of this highly educated man, and it was indeed the favor of God that he is alive today. Sometimes we would be stopped by police on the short drive from my apartment on one side of town to the medical school campus on the other side of Baltimore. This was a reminder of the stereotype that a Black man driving could not possibly be a medical student at one of the world's most prestigious institutions. After those times, I'd hold him and allow the emotions to simmer down. We would shift the focus to the work that still needed to be done for racial justice. A small consolation is that the discovery that he was not a Black man driving a stolen car shattered every stereotype that the police officer had constructed. It was a minor victory.

HOP #5: We'd find the things to be thankful for, and we believed that there would be change! We had built a Scaffold of Positivity even back then.

Our relationship blossomed and grew, with years and years of experiences that would take volumes to capture: road trips, celebrations, challenges, carnivals, dance parties, picnics, cookouts, family reunions, and golf trips. Our home became the hub for family, friends, medical students, and residents in training, and we advanced in our purpose of caring for patients in the way God had called us to. We were blessed, and favor was upon our lives. Like every relationship, we had some rocky roads. The first two years that I was in medical school were probably the toughest. It was my first jaunt at maintaining a long-distance relationship, and it was not easy. We had also both transitioned to new places—I had moved to Boston and Charles to DC. Charles had graduated to a BMW. His Mazda RX7 was stolen in NYC during one of his visits to Gary, and that BMW, along with his MD degree, marked him as a desirable mate for many! When I look back, even then, I was exercising HOP #5—I'd found things in our relationship to be thankful for and believed that if we were supposed to be together, it would eventually work out.

Of course, we did encounter some drama before I could reach that mature conclusion! Remember back when there were landlines where each phone number called was itemized on the statement? Well, there was a recurring number that I did not recognize, and I called said number because I was a self-appointed private investigator! My recommendation is that if you are ever in that situation, don't call the number if you don't want to hear information that might be painful! The number belonged to a woman with a car name like Mercedes or Lexus, who told me it was open season since I was in another city. It was like a punch in the gut, but I eventually picked myself up off the floor and faced the harsh reality that sometimes you have to let things go and trust that they will return to you if it was meant to be.

We took a break from each other during my first year of medical school, and I can genuinely say that it was the best thing that happened to our relationship. Even though I didn't have my Habit of Positivity #5 fully activated at the time of that telephone call, I can look back and be very thankful that we had that hiatus! We came back together knowing that we were meant for each other. Positivity Posse, how many times do we feel that if we hold on, things will work out? Whether it's friendships, lovers, dysfunctional jobs, or material things? I've come to understand more and more that we can only control how we think, how we feel, the choices we make and the actions we take. Beyond that, we have to let go and find places of gratitude. It has been 35 years since we met at that pool party, 29 married, and Charles and I are still each other's best friends and champions. Whether it is as a cameraman, IT consultant, tent erector, or book salesman, Charles has stood by steadfastly, letting my light shine. When the spotlight is on me, he is not in the least bit daunted by the shadow that it sometimes casts on him, in the same way, that when his light is shining brightly, and I stand in the shadows cheering him on. We truly HOPped into favor in our partnership.

Seeing the Favor in My Positivity Window

Being a doctor can be a double-edged sword, especially when taking care of family. I've always felt incredibly thankful to be a resource and advocate for family and friends, especially in a healthcare environment where unconscious bias is real. But it comes at a cost. In the same way that we carry our patient concerns with us, it is magnified when a family member or friend is ill. Imagine what happens when your child or spouse has an issue. It can be the worst feeling, as you think about all the things that can go wrong. How many of you have ever had a premature child or a sick child admitted to the hospital? If you have, I know you will appreciate what I am talking about.

After years of infertility, our son Mark was born just shy of 32 weeks. It was unbelievably difficult. Because we had lost his twin brother earlier in the pregnancy, I was so afraid that Mark would not make it. I was pulling out my hair with worry as he lay in the incubator. He was so tiny and helpless, and I was terrified he would have some awful complications. I had absolutely no control, and I was driving myself crazy with worry. The only way that I survived was by forcing myself to regroup. I had to hold my hand up several times a day and say "Not today" to fear, worry, and anxiety. I had to focus on HOP #5—I'd find things in each day to be thankful for and believe that he was going to be okay. Ultimately, the only thing that we can be sure of is what is happening in the present. What we choose to believe about the future affects how we feel in the present. By choosing to believe that Mark would be fine helped me embrace the present with joy and hope.

I had to look at my Positivity Scaffold and deal with what was in front of me, each little win at a time. I gave thanks, looked through the Positivity Window, and saw the favor. I saw how the tiny solutions all added up to address the big problems.

I kept forcing myself to look through my Positivity Window, framed by the Habits of Positivity, to see how I already had so much favor in the situation. We had a ton of support and my husband was a neonatologist, so the favor doesn't get much better than that! What is the likelihood that we would have ready access to everything we needed to understand what was happening with our son because that was my husband's specialty? Unlimited favor. He helped me believe that there was a solution (HOP #1). He helped me extract the positives in the situation (HOP #3): As our son gained weight one gram at a time, every cc of milk intake became a reason for celebration. Charles helped me see all the little details in the background that I had to be thankful for. It was my husband, the neonatologist, who calmed and reassured me and framed everything through our Life Window to see God's unlimited favor in our lives.

Sometimes the favor in your life is invisible until you apply the situation to your Positivity Scaffold.

The perspective shift is like putting film through the developer, revealing the favor, and recognizing that you have access to a lot more than you think. During a crisis, it is challenging to have that perspective. Identify your person that can help you look through your Positivity Window and keep them on speed dial!

Have you ever heard the saying, "Lightning never strikes the same place twice?" That's a myth! In actuality, lightning striking the same place is the norm rather than the exception. So when my husband's prostate blood test rose ever so slightly, and his primary-care doctor dismissed it as no reason for concern. As the urologist wife, I insisted we follow the levels more closely. The trend continued, and I asked one of my mentors to evaluate him. Even though I knew lightning could strike the same place twice, never in my wildest dreams would I have imagined that my healthy, 48-year-old husband would be diagnosed with prostate cancer. As he looked at me to make sense of this diagnosis, the vulnerability and fear in his eyes must have been the exact look that I had in my eyes, as I looked to him to be reassured when our son was in the NICU. Were we really in this place again, except with the roles reversed? We dragged ourselves to our Positivity Window and saw the unlimited favor in the sky. We had to practice HOP #5—to be thankful for the blessing, even amid the challenge, and believe we had everything we needed. The early pickup was made because I am a urologist.

I lived with a pit in my stomach right until the day of his surgery. The kind of pit that turns and twists to the point of nausea. Every time that fear and worry tried to creep in, I would have to raise my hand and say, "Not today." We had to put every positive expectation into the atmosphere. I kept looking through our window, framed by the Habits of

Positivity, recognizing the favor, even though the sky was stormy. Charles' surgery was performed by my mentor, whom I trusted implicitly—favor. I was surrounded by a village of women who loved me and distracted me in the surgical waiting room—favor. His pathology showed the tumor was localized to the prostate—favor. He spent one night in the hospital, and the rest of his post-op care was done at home by his personal urologist—favor. He had no complications and returned to full functioning—favor. I shifted from being a urologist to the wife of a man with prostate cancer that threatened the up-end seat of his manhood. Suddenly, I was up close and personal with the deep vulnerabilities that my patients and their partners face. The expanded layers of intimacy and partnership that developed between Charles and me on his road to recovery positioned me to be more than a urologist for my patients in ways that I would have never imagined- the unlimited favor of God in our lives.

In both experiences, it would have been easy to allow negativity to drive a spiral of fear, self-pity, frustration, anger, disappointment, worry, discontent, and feelings of lack. Instead, by launching a counterattack with our HOP artillery and clearing a path to our Positivity Window, we could look out onto our Sky of Favor and cope and hope during this unsettling time. We led the charge with HOP #5: Being thankful and believing. The more we planted gratitude, the less room was available for negative emotions to germinate and grow.

Appreciating Favor in the Moments—Even in a Painful Outcome

As doctors, we are wired to be problem solvers. Sometimes, even without being asked to solve the problem, we jump in with "unsolicited advice." We can't help ourselves! That is how it was with Loretta, the sister of one of my closest friends. A ray of sunshine with a ready smile and infectious laugh, she had been battling leukemia for two years. Initially treated in the Caribbean, she responded to treatment and went into remission. All seemed well for a year. Then the cancer returned and did not respond to repeat treatments. It was serendipity that I called my friend Claudia on the day that the doctor told Loretta he had no other interventions to offer. It was a routine check-in call, and I was unaware of what had transpired with Loretta's condition. As I casually asked about the entire family, including Loretta, I could hear the terror in my friend's voice as she tried to process the new reality they were confronting. Before I could activate the feedback loop between my mouth and brain, my Habits of Positivity exploded on the scene, and I heard myself say, "I know there is a solution; let me work to help find it." (HOP #1)

After my declaration, time became a whirlwind—a flurry of divine appointments and connections, calls to doctors, paperwork, and insurance approvals, resulting in an expedited appointment at our cancer center. Loretta's white blood cell count was extremely high, and her other blood counts relatively low, so she needed medications and transfusions to get her blood numbers to a level where it would be safe for her to travel.

Infection and bleeding were the main concerns. Loretta had a 24- to 48-hour window to travel to the US after receiving those treatments before the levels become abnormal again. As unimaginable as it might seem, Loretta arrived in Boston and checked into a world-class hospital one week after I made that check-in call to my friend.

You might say to yourself, "So why is this a big deal?" Loretta was coming from a developing country with limited health insurance to cover the US's astronomical cost of care, and she had no immediate access to other health coverage. Typically, one has to show proof of paying for the out-of-pocket costs before making an appointment. Yet, in a dire and terminal situation, it was the launching of the Positivity Power with a declaration of "I can" that paved the way for hope. It was truly miraculous and a manifestation of incredible favor how all the pieces fell into place to allow for such a quick response.

The only treatment option remaining was a bone marrow transplant, which is a lengthy process. I immediately volunteered that she and her sister could stay with our family. On the day of their arrival, I drove to the airport early. The trip had been a long haul, and Loretta was visibly tired. She walked slowly toward the car, her mask obscuring the effort etched on her face. Claudia and I assisted her gently into the car, covering her with a blanket, as it was fall in New England and a sharp nip was in the air. I could feel her frail, bony frame below my fingers, and I wasn't prepared for how ill she looked. Gaunt with a wan complexion and haunted look in her eyes, she took down her mask and flashed me the million-dollar smile that was her signature. Despite my heartache at her appearance, I saw the joy and gratitude in her soul to have successfully crossed the ocean for a chance to hope, a chance to believe, a chance to live. She rested at our home overnight, and we took her to the hospital the following morning.

The first admission lasted 10 days, and after discharge, Loretta settled into our guest room, requiring antibiotic infusions every eight hours to treat an infection in her blood. Initially, I did the infusions until Claudia could get comfortable. A few nights after their arrival, as I lay reading a bedtime story to my 11-year-old son and hearing the soft murmur of voices in the adjoining guest room, a wave of fear suddenly overcame me. Mark had lost his grandfather and nanny within the previous three years, and I wondered about the psychological impact if Loretta were to die. Had I been too hasty? Pushing down the rising tide of fear and putting my hand up to block debilitating anxiety, I kept repeating, "Not today, fear. Not today."

As scared as I was, I was reminded that I was not the author, the director, or the producer of this script. I was merely an actor and needed to do my part. Negativity is always lurking to derail divine assignments. I looked through my Positivity Window at the Sky of Favor: Loretta needed a new medication that had been approved for broader use three months before her arrival—favor. Loretta's insurance had a cap, which would have disqualified her if recognized by the hospital before her arrival - favor. Once that insurance limit was recognized, treatment with the new medication cost $100,000 per dose was put on hold. This was a major crisis as she had been responding well to the medication. After many calls, conversations, and amazing advocates, Loretta qualified for a program where the medication would be provided for free as long as she needed it—favor. How could we not practice HOP #5—Being Thankful and Believing? During this challenging circumstance, focusing on gratitude kept moving us toward hope.

Loretta's only child was a freshman at a nearby university. While it was devastating to have the disease recur, had Loretta remained in the Caribbean, she would have likely succumbed before her daughter could see her. During her treatment, Loretta's daughter and other family members spent a lot of time with her at our home, helping to care for her, bonding and spending quality time that our sometimes-hectic lives do not permit—favor. As the treatment unfolded and the cancer responded, there was another stumbling block: how the bone marrow transplant would be paid for. The cancer was in remission, and a cure seemed within reach, except the insurance had run out. It was frustrating and nerve-wracking, and emotions were raw. In those times, we had to pause and pivot to HOP #5—Staying thankful and believing.

We had to keep looking out our Positivity Window, remembering how far we had come so that we could consciously choose gratitude. Loretta had been at death's door when she arrived, and now she had responded to the medication, had no significant complications, and was feeling and looking much better—favor. Loretta had an army of prayer warriors encamped around her, and the situation called on us to lean on what we knew—HOP #5: Be thankful and believe. Believe that all things are possible with God and lo-and-behold, the additional insurance for which Loretta had applied was approved, as was the Bone Marrow Transplant—favor. When we are in the middle of difficult times, we often become impatient and develop amnesia. We have to say "Not today" to impatience and forgetting our blessings and apply our Positivity Scaffold situation. Then we can see exactly how far we have come.

My friend Claudia was Loretta's right-hand person, keeping track of all the moving parts and administrative processes so Loretta could focus on staying positive—favor. The young lady who made the mistake of approving Loretta's visit had no regrets. For her, the positives of offering Loretta a chance to beat her disease far outweighed the negatives (HOP #3) —favor. Loretta had at least one family member or friend who stayed with her and became a part of our family during the six months before her bone marrow treatment. Despite the diagnosis, they were upbeat, brought much joy and laughter to our home, and our family was greatly enriched—favor.

Loretta had a strong faith and joy that overflowed, even on her worst days. She loved connection and tradition and introduced forgotten recipes, old-time stories, and new perspectives on things we often took for granted. Loretta and her friends would sit at the kitchen table and survey the drama unfolding between the chipmunks, squirrels, and hawks in our backyard. They were privy to an entire production of stolen acorns, territorial battles, and fascinating romances because of their quiet observation. They delighted in regaling us with the day's episode. She was pure inspiration.

I knew that Loretta's pathology was unfavorable—even with the bone marrow transplant, there were no guarantees of a cure—but the most important thing was to enjoy each day as a gift and not to skip forward to things over which we had no control. If we allow ourselves to get to a place of complete surrender, it enables us to let go of any responsibility for the outcome. When we relinquish that responsibility, the gift is the freedom to stay in the moment. It can be challenging but practicing gratitude at the moment helps to keep us there.

Loretta had the bone marrow transplant six months after she arrived in Boston. She was a star patient whose quick wit, ready smile, and positive attitude endeared her to all the staff. So compelling was her personality that she became a spokesperson on one of the hospital videos, describing her experience as a bone marrow patient. I remember how our home exploded with hope when we learned that Loretta's daughter would be her bone marrow donor. Bone marrow transplants are often fraught with delays because of the intricacies of controlling for infection while wiping out the body's immune system. Establishing the new donor immune system is a delicate balance. The process was no different for Loretta, but it was as if the bright light of the impending transplant could not be dimmed, and there was an extra pep in all of our steps, especially Loretta's, as we marched through the process together. Finally, the transplant was complete. A seemingly straightforward infusion of what looked like a bag of blood belied the complexity of the pre-transplant and post-transplant processes.

Loretta was discharged one month after her transplant to a wonderful apartment that the family had found so she could recover in a more controlled environment. She was gaining strength, responding well, and enjoying the burgeoning signs of Spring when the winds were knocked out of our sails during a doctor visit. The cancer had returned, and that was a bad sign. Our skies immediately became dark and stormy, and we were so devastated, disappointed, and sad. It was tough to look through the Positivity Window. It was such a huge letdown. However, Loretta did not give up. She pulled herself together, put on her bravest smile, and nudged us all to the Positivity Window. She focused on being thankful that the doctors were not giving up either and they were going to pursue every avenue for treatment. Despite all the efforts, the cancer was unrelenting, and Loretta died four months later. How can one possibly find the positives when the outcome was not what we had hoped and prayed for? The pain of the loss was deep and almost unbearable. Yet, we could feel her presence comforting and encouraging us. As we invited more and more of the perspective of not what we lost but what we kept, we could find moments of peace, joy, and gratitude. We gave thanks to how we had Loretta for ten months longer than if she had stayed in the Caribbean.

The opportunities for fellowship and treasured memories that were created were invaluable. We had so much to be thankful for. We stopped and looked through the Positivity Window at what we learned from Loretta. We marveled at all the favor, love, care, and companionship showered on Loretta during the last year of her life and knew that that experience filled her up. She transitioned, surrounded by her female armor-bearers, who formed a chain link of prayer around her and gently, lovingly, and reassuringly whispered to her that all was well. As she entered her heavenly home, she knew she was well-loved and that she was leaving a legacy of love that will live on for generations. And so, we gave thanks again.

How often have we found ourselves in situations where we wanted an outcome so badly that when things didn't go the way we hoped or expected, we were devastated? This is especially true in a health crisis where a loved one does not survive. Our minds immediately flip to what could have been done differently. Sometimes we blame ourselves. Sometimes we blame others. Sometimes we ask why God would allow this to happen. The grief and loss torment us, and we cannot accept that that person's physical presence is gone.

If we see ourselves as physical beings, as well as a life force, that create impact and change, we shift our perspective about loss. Let me nerd out for a minute! Stay with me! Force is defined as "mass x acceleration." So one might ask, "How can force be felt if the mass (the physical body) is not there?" Let's look beyond the equation and focus on the definition of force as "an interaction between objects that causes them to change motion!" Suppose you think of your loved one's life force as an interaction that caused a change in you, then their force continues. The legacy that he or she has left you guides your thinking and behavior so the life force of your loved one is alive and well in you. This can help you pivot to Habit of Positivity #5: Be thankful and believe.

When you experience losing a loved one, look through your Positivity Window at all the blessings that person brought to your life (favor) and reflect on how it helped you change. This activity will always propel you to a place of gratitude. It doesn't take away the sting of sadness or disappointment, but it creates the opportunity not to be defeated by them.

POSITIVITY PAUSE

How often do you walk by a window and not look through it? Think of favor as equivalent to the sky—no matter where you are in the world, the sky is always present. You just have to step closer to the window and look out and up. We have unlimited access to favor, but it requires action. We have to make a mental shift. The Habits of Positivity frame the window—it invites us to look out and up. Does the sky always look the same? No. Sometimes the sky will be cloudy with thunderclouds or sometimes it will be clear and bright blue. Sometimes it is ablaze with the variegated oranges of a brilliant sunset or has a muted glow as the sun rises. Sometimes it is awash with twinkling, playful stars or looks like a velvety blanket of a black bear's fur. The appearance of the sky reflects the situations in our life. Whatever the circumstance, favor, like the sky, is always there. The presentation and package of favor come in all different appearances. What does that mean for you? Positivity Windows are at your fingertips because you can build one wherever you are. Just construct your Positivity Frame with your 5 Habits of Positivity and look out and up and see the expansive favor spread before you.

POSITIVITY PRACTICE

Look Through Your Positivity Window

1. Meditate on what your Positivity Window looks like.

2. Look through your Positivity Window and reflect on what the sky looks like today.

3. Reflect on experiences when the skies have been bright.

4. Reflect on experiences when the skies have been dark.

5. Sit for 10 minutes every day with your HOP frame, apply the Habits of Positivity to experiences from the day, and list the favor you could identify in each situation.

TRANSFORMATION

Reflect on the differences when you didn't notice the favor in your Positivity Window versus how you feel looking through your Positivity Window with the Habits of Positivity as the frame. Journal your responses below:

Before I started looking through my Positivity Window, I used to feel:

Now that I look through my Positivity Window, framed by the Habits of Positivity and see the Sky of Favor daily, I feel:

CHAPTER 11

Unlimited Faith—
Life Staircase

"Now FAITH is the substance of things hoped for, the evidence of things not seen."

—HEBREWS 11:1

"Don't be afraid—if you are afraid you can't move forward."

—MALALA YOUSAFZAI

HOW IS YOUR FAITH MOST often challenged? When do you find yourself struggling to believe because you don't see things happening immediately and right in front of you? How many times do you want to see significant results and miss the small steps that start your journey? How often do you fall prey to the unbelief the negativity monster sows in you, which then takes root like killer weeds, multiplying at warp speed and strangling any fruit-bearing plants in you? Can you build your faith by climbing your Life Staircase, using the Habits of Positivity to put down one tread at a time? Yes, you can!

In this chapter, I'll share a story about how I nearly allowed my fear to sideline my faith and how I used my Habits of Positivity to defeat negativity. I'll show you how sometimes reflecting on your past can bolster your faith, as you acknowledge all the moments when you were able to manifest your hopes and dreams, even if it wasn't exactly in the way you had initially envisioned.

Climbing My Life Staircase Toward Faith

How many of you have watched medical TV dramas and thought the scenarios seemed far-fetched? As a physician, sometimes I have scoffed out loud! If I had seen my story on TV, I would have dismissed the scenario as completely made up. To give you a little background, I live close to downtown Boston, and at the time of this story, I was in private practice and operated at a hospital forty-five minutes from Boston. It was midafternoon on a routine operating day, and I was performing my final surgery of the day. The last thing that I remember was the world spinning around me and then turning pitch black. When I opened my eyes, the world slowly coming back into focus, I was looking directly into my patient's eyes. *What in the world? Was I really staring into the eyes of the patient who I had just operated on?* I looked around me, seeing the recovery room stretchers lined up like soldiers with soft fluorescent lights casting shadows on the nurses positioned like sentinels at their stations.

"Dr. Williams, Dr. Williams, are you awake? You fainted in the operating room." The nursing supervisor's anxious voice pierced my fog.

My anesthesia colleague interjected, "Oneeka, you passed out as you removed the cystoscope from your patient's bladder. He's doing fine."

Somehow my colleague knew that my first concern would be for my patient. How many of you do the same thing? Always think of others before yourself?

It all came flooding back to me. The pain had started midway through the surgery. I could feel a searing ache on the right side of my abdomen, alerting me that something was not right. I shifted position, adjusting the protective lead apron under my sterile gown, hoping that the pain would wane. It did not. Sometimes we can ignore our body and the reality unfolding right in front of us. Doctors do it, too! By sheer force of will, like a finger plugging the hole of a dike, with massive waves of a category-five hurricane pounding, I focused on my patient. I moved efficiently but urgently through the rest of the procedure, denying my brain the acknowledgment of the inferno erupting on my insides. Stone obstructing the ureter fragmented, ensnared in a basket, and retrieved, a stent in the ureter placed, cystoscope removed from the bladder. Then, the dike broke, and the darkness enveloped me.

The anesthesiologist asked, "Do you have any idea why you would have fainted? Your blood pressure is quite low. We've placed an I.V. and are giving you some fluids."

"How long have I been out?" I asked.

"It's only been a few minutes," he replied. "Any idea why you would have fainted?" he repeated.

As a matter of fact, I had a very good idea. This was the continuing saga of our fertility journey. You will recollect the pregnancy and delivery stories in earlier chapters, but this is some of what came before: cycle number three of in vitro fertilization (IVF). Somehow, I always suspected that getting pregnant was not easy for me. I had terrible menstrual cramps as a teenager and vividly remembered being carted out of the all-boys school I attended almost every month. During medical school and residency, my cycles were so severe and disruptive that I started continuous birth control pills to shut them down completely. I could not imagine how I could survive training if I did not show up for work because I was sick. I wondered if I had set myself up because of my negative expectations and had somehow spoken them into existence. We have to be so conscious of what we put into the universe, as that energy can manifest in many ways.

We have to look for the pattern of positives and successes in our lives and use those to frame our expectations.

The Scaffold of Positivity helps you to do this as you climb your Life Staircase toward faith.

Sometimes life comes at you in ways you never imagined, making the challenges you had previously experienced seem like a walk in the park! Have you ever planned your life in a stepwise fashion? You've probably heard the famous Benjamin Franklin quote, "If you fail to plan, you are planning to fail," but we rarely take the added measure to determine whose plan we are referencing. God's plan never fails, but the human plan is never guaranteed. Have you ever put your time and effort into building and preparing, moving from phase to phase, and then arriving at a place where you found yourself running into one roadblock after another? That is how it was for our fertility journey.

Training as a surgeon was so rigorous that we waited until I completed residency to start a family. But then it wasn't so easy. We became the godparents to so many of our friends who seemed to have children with no difficulty, and it felt as if I planned or co-hosted every one of their baby showers. It was kind of like being the perpetual bridesmaid! One strategy for dealing with hardships is connecting to the meaning in your life by caring for others, which takes the focus off of your hardship. HOP #4 references that our purpose is linked to caring for others. With each baby shower, I would climb my Life Staircase toward faith and keep stepping up, focusing on all that I was thankful for, including the new life we were celebrating. I would believe that if God could do it for others, He would surely do it for me. But there were tough days when I would feel discouraged and ask why it seemed like the one thing that we wanted most was out of our reach. I would wallow under the covers for a little while; then I'd have to revive my spunk, put my hand up to discouragement and unbelief and say, "Not today!"

I remember one New Year's Eve, sitting with our family and reflecting on our hopes for the upcoming year. I broke down in my mom's arms, wracked with sobs as I asked why God had forsaken me. She reminded me I was God's precious child, and for as much as I had allowed God to use me to bless others, my time would surely come. She took me by the hand, stepped onto the Life Staircase with me, and reminded me I was highly favored, and she had faith that we would have a child. Sometimes, when your faith is not powerful enough, there is someone who will bolster your faith with their own. In that simple declaration, she reminded me to be thankful and keep believing (HOP #5).

By releasing my pent-up frustration, it was as if I released the negativity, disappointments, and anger, which cleared the way for me to have renewed hope. Sometimes we don't recognize how many blessings and provisions are in our lives because we are so focused on what we don't have—the lack—rather than what we have. We become so inundated with the negatives of our experiences—the things that subtract from us—that we miss the positives or those things that add to us. This is because we haven't layered the experiences on our Positivity Scaffolds.

By stepping onto my Life Staircase, I was reminded that faith is an incredible gift: the substance of things hoped for and the evidence of things not seen. We just have to lift our feet and lay down our positivity treads one at a time. We are not just climbing a staircase that we cannot see; we are laying down the treads, building the staircase as we believe and climb in faith. Even during the most challenging points in our lives, the Positivity Scaffolds create the frame to cope and build bridges to hope.

Finally, after trying unsuccessfully to become pregnant, we started our fertility treatment journey three years post-residency. It was far more eventful than what I imagined. Frankly, I hadn't given the process much thought. I just took the bull by the horns in standard fashion, as I was squeezing all the visits and procedures in between patient surgeries and clinics, so I had no time to think. The assisted reproductive process occurs in phases. The first phase is to administer medication to stimulate the production of eggs from the ovaries. Next, sperm is inserted directly into the uterus to coincide with the eggs' release. This is called Intrauterine Insemination (IUI). I remember my first scheduled intrauterine insemination cycle. My ovaries made so many eggs that we had to switch to an in vitro fertilization (IVF) cycle where eggs were harvested under anesthesia and combined with the sperm in a petri dish so that the embryos can develop and then be transferred into the uterus. This was done because the overstimulation of the ovary resulted in the release of so many eggs that could have made me quite ill. I remember thinking, *I am such an overachiever,* producing far more eggs than expected! But, alas, despite the number of eggs, we did not have a successful IVF cycle, so we returned to trying IUI cycles twice more before we moved back to in vitro fertilization. The second IVF cycle was unsuccessful, and we started a third cycle.

After transferring two embryos, we waited with bated breath for the first Beta-hCG pregnancy blood test, praying that it would be positive. Have you ever noticed that time slows down when you are waiting for something really important to you? I was counting the minutes and pouring positive affirmations, energy, and thoughts into my reproductive tract. The call that the Beta-hCG was positive came while I was at work. My heart leaped in a thrilling rapid sequence, but the nurse's following statement tempered this: "It's not as high as we would like to see, but this can happen, so we will have to wait for the next blood tests." I refused to be discouraged by those ominous words. "Focus on faith," I told myself.

Have you ever had to give yourself injections? The pain depends on needle size, the depth of the injection, and the fluid that is being injected. If the needle is small, the injection superficial, and the fluid thin and not irritating, the injection is unlikely to hurt. The hormone given to support an embryo's growth is dissolved in thick oil, so the needles need to be pretty big. The injection is given in the butt and hurts like the dickens! However, I had happily become a regular pincushion. There can be a lot of truth to the adage "no pain, no gain," so during this time, I cheerfully continued daily hormone injections to help the embryo grow. Follow-up blood tests revealed that the Beta-hCG was not rising as rapidly as it should, which my doctor interpreted as the embryo not being viable. The other possibility was that the pregnancy could be ectopic (outside the womb). Neither sounded good. I had an ultrasound, which couldn't locate the embryo inside or outside the uterus (because it was still too early), but they told me to stop the hormone shots.

But we don't know what's going on because we saw nothing, I thought. I agonized over that instruction because I had already formed an attachment to the kernel of life within me. Was it impossible things could improve? Would I be withdrawing the lifeline that the embryo needed to grow? As irrational as it may sound, I could not bring myself to stop the shots. Yes, I admit it! I was doing the very thing that I know drives me, as a physician, crazy: not listening to the experts' recommendations! Unfortunately, this is a familiar theme during these pandemic times. Sadly, it hasn't ended well for the country, and it didn't end well for me either. The Beta-hCG numbers kept inching up, and I kept waiting for the miracle. I continued the hormone shots. I held on to my faith, which brings us back to the fateful day in the operating room, four weeks after the first Beta-hCG result.

I said to my anesthesia colleague, "I just started an IVF cycle, and we need to rule out an ectopic pregnancy."

I was whisked to the ultrasound department with lightning speed, and a large collection was seen near my right fallopian tube. I was mortified to be carted through the hospital hallways as the staff whispered and wondered what was wrong with me! The bleeding seemed to have stopped, but I needed surgery. My doctor was at another hospital an hour away, and because I was stable, a helicopter transported me to the hospital in Boston for surgery.

It was surreal—the frenzy of activity and the fact that I was now a patient experiencing a life-threatening emergency. I still could not get out of my compulsive caretaking role. I was trying to juggle and manage the flow of information to my doctor, extremely anxious husband and my partners (to follow up and care for the patient I operated on) without speaking directly to any of them.

As we flew toward Boston, amidst the noise of the helicopter engines, which was only slightly louder than my heartbeat, I wondered how the heck I ended up here! Was I in the twilight zone? I was beating myself up, asking myself if I had delayed starting a family for too long. Had I put surgical training ahead of my family? Had I made too big a sacrifice? It was a bad idea to doctor myself. Would this have happened if I had stopped the shots? I needed to put my hand up to all the negative thought patterns, focus on placing my Habits of Positivity on my Life Staircase, and hold on to faith. I knew that my attitude going into this surgery was critical. I had to focus on HOP #5—to be thankful that things were stable and believe that I would be okay.

I had had surgeries before, but never emergency surgery. As my surgeon reviewed all the potential complications—the need to convert to open surgery, risk of loss of ovary and/or tube, uncontrolled bleeding, risk of death—I felt terrified at being in a position of having absolutely no control. I wondered if this was how my patients felt when I reviewed their consent forms with them.

He took my hand (as I often do with my patients), he looked into my eyes (as I often do with my patients), and he said (as I often say to my patients), "I will take good care of you."

I have not experienced many times where I have feared for my life. When I first felt the pain in the O.R., I had that sickening feeling that something was going wrong. I was nervous and in the depths of despair about whether I would bleed to death, lose some of my reproductive organs, or suffer some crazy complications. It's almost Murphy's Law that if you are a physician-patient, you can expect the unexpected. How many of us caregivers think of how the situation affects those around us before we think of ourselves? Well, that was me. I truly worried about how my family would be affected if something happened to me. I had jumped all the way ahead, creating a false narrative of an outcome in my head. I had allowed the negativity monster to instill fear in my heart: False Evidence Appearing Real.

As I lay in the pre-op area awaiting my surgery, my vitals were stable, my head clear, and I had to launch my Habits of

Positivity to defeat that monster. I put my hand right in its face and declared, "Not today!" I thought of the Habits of Positivity as being the substance of faith, and I just needed to lay them down one tread at a time on my Life Staircase and focus on the tread—the HOP—right in front of me, and step on that one before laying down the next one. I had to believe that I would get to a destination one step at a time. Those steps build the staircase, and you can turn and look back at them and see the positivity form. But you have to step first, believing that the tread is there. Bend your knee and lift your leg; the tread appears as if the action of raising your leg in faith induces the tread or provision.

Faith is the substance of things hoped for and the evidence of things unseen. I had the substance and the evidence of how my higher power, God, was working on my behalf, and I had to let go and lean into faith. I had to close my eyes, block out all negative thoughts, and just focus on my breathing. You actually can't deep breathe and have thoughts racing through your head at the same time. It cuts your breath short.

There has been nothing about me or my life that has followed a script! When I woke up after surgery, I remember seeing my surgeon smiling, which was enough to calm my nerves. Not surprisingly, my laparoscopic exploration findings were that I had a ruptured ectopic pregnancy, but the embryo had gone rogue! Instead of implanting in the fallopian tubes, the most common location for ectopic pregnancies, the embryo had exited the tubes and implanted one of the ligaments that support the uterus. I felt as if I had won the lottery!

I embraced HOP #5: Be thankful and believe! I had been so sick with worry that I would have a complicated surgery that when my surgeon told me I did not lose my ovary or my tube, and I was very much alive, I felt an enormous wave of relief and gratitude! The patient I had been operating on when I fainted also did well and I was very thankful. Once the dust settled, I could feel the heavy weight of sadness. When was it going to be my time? However, even though I did not have a "successful pregnancy," I could still shift from disappointment to embracing the blessings in the experience. You better believe that I learned a lot of valuable lessons! I had to force myself to take inventory. I made a list. Positivity does not mean looking at yourself through rose-colored glasses and not being honest with yourself. I could be vulnerable with myself and acknowledge my role in the situation. I could learn from that, which is a positive, and let go of the self-critique once I had extracted and processed the lesson.

This journey felt like no matter how hard I tried, I was failing. This was a first for me because I believed that the harder one worked, the more likely one could achieve one's goals. That had always worked for me. I believed I had control of the outcome based on what I put in. I depended on my plan, and it was utterly destabilizing to feel as if nothing I was doing worked. There was almost a sense of shame that accompanied our infertility, as if it somehow reflected on me. I often see this thinking play out in my patients and community—the sense of shame or feelings of inadequacy that accompany a medical diagnosis. You play back in your head all the things you could or should have done differently, which can paralyze you even further. Somehow you blame yourself for the situation, and in those quiet moments, you probably think you got what you deserved. Then one of two things can happen:

- You deny the issue and bury your head in the sand to avoid the psychological conflict that comes with assigning responsibility to yourself, and the condition worsens and continues to reinforce the narrative of blame and shame,

OR

- You reach for a scaffold that helps you get out of bed, and using one Habit of Positivity at a time, you deconstruct the challenge and rebuild on the HOP scaffold.

Sometimes it's tough to do the work by yourself, especially if you've become so discouraged that any platitudes from well-meaning family and friends just irritate you.

So, what can you do? Here's what I recommend:

- Get a HOP partner—someone you trust. When we sit with fears in our head and heart, we are unwilling to voice the concern because we believe we give life to events if we articulate them. So, they fester on the inside. Release and deactivate them. It reminds me of skeet shooting, where you have to release the target before you can destroy it. A HOP partner is a safe space, someone who you trust and respect, who allows you to verbalize fears and then helps you apply the problem to the HOP scaffold. The perspective that emerges from this practice will release you from fear.

- Talk about the loss. Don't hide from the sadness, the disappointments, the dashed hopes, the pain, the feelings of lack, or the hopelessness. Identify the feelings, name them, and process them. Then, apply the experience to the scaffold to identify the parts of the experience that strengthened you, contributed to your growth, and allow gratitude to wash over you. Eventually, gratitude will become more dominant, and it will lessen the sting of loss and sadness.

Why did the embryo take an errant journey into my abdomen? No one knows. We took time to understand the problem before identifying potential solutions. (Refer to Chapter 2 for the Anatomy of a Problem exercise in HOP #1.) I had large uterine fibroids surgically removed after that experience. Even though there has been much debate about whether fibroids contribute to infertility and pregnancy loss, anecdotal evidence suggests that they do contribute. It was the one thing that we could fix, given that my fibroids had significantly increased in size during the fertility stimulation. I had an open myomectomy to remove 33 fibroids, and the IVF cycle after my fibroid surgery resulted in Matthew and Mark's twin pregnancy. This time I followed instructions to the letter of the law and had a successful pregnancy, and we now have a healthy 15-year-old son!

Another blessing for which I am so thankful, is that this experience opened up my mind to consider alternative therapies in a way that I never had before. I had spent no time thinking about the mind, body, and spirit connection in my medical and surgical training. I initially started acupuncture to create alignment during my IVF cycles, and then I used it to control the pregnancy symptoms of migraines and nausea. I was blown away by this 3,000-year-old modality that can tap into the body's natural pathways to achieve healing. I understood how it is an essential element of maintaining our health and wellness. It created such an indelible impact, that my husband and I later opened two acupuncture clinics because we wanted to make access to this amazing medicine easier and more affordable for patients. We kept laying down the HOP treads on our Life Staircase and having faith—we kept stepping on the evidence of things hoped for and the substance of things unseen.

How many times do you struggle with faith? You know the saying that, "Seeing is believing." It is so much easier to believe the things that we can see, and therefore we look ahead into the future to try to see the outcome so that we can believe it is possible. While we can visualize the future in our mind's eye, we cannot extract evidence from the future. Faith requires that we trust what we know from the past that gives us hope for the future. And so, if "Seeing is believing," we should be able to look back in our lives and find those places that provide the substance of things hoped for. How many times have you reflected on things that you had hoped for and saw that they were manifested, sometimes in ways that you did not expect? Those experiences allow you to position your Habits of Positivity treads on to your Life Staircase and demonstrate the power within you as you choose to exercise your faith.

I imagine some of you reading this book did not have the successful pregnancy outcome—or a positive outcome to whatever you hoped for—and you wonder how you can cope and hope when things did not turn out the way you wanted. We did not have a successful second pregnancy despite multiple attempts and losses, so I understand that position as well. It becomes even more critical for you to apply the Positivity Scaffold. It's the only way to gain insights that help you focus on the journey and not the destination. Here's my advice:

- Be open that there will be solutions, maybe just not the ones you envisioned.

- Explore how the challenges or limits have created opportunities.

- Learn the discipline of sorting through the positives and negatives, process the negatives, but then do not hold on to them so that they continue to subtract from you.

- Find the meaning and assignments in these experiences and parlay them into helping others.

- Identify all the things you can be thankful for despite the outcome, making room for you to believe that there is hope.

POSITIVITY PAUSE

How can you climb your Life Staircase toward faith when you do not know what is at the top of those stairs? It simply starts with believing! Believing does not mean that you must have the entire vision in your head and a clear sense of what is at the top of the staircase. It simply means that you believe that as you raise your leg to take the following steps, the tread will be laid down. Faith is activating the muscles to lift your leg. You decide based on the belief that the tread will be laid down and ready for you to step onto it. The Habits of Positivity as the treads are important because they are all attached to a conscious choice or active shift in thinking. This is what faith is about—the substance is the action you will take to express your belief. Stepping on each tread keeps you present. It removes an attachment to the outcome and brings the focus squarely back to what you can do now.

Even for those of us who have deep faith, the negativity monster still prowls. My faith was tested, and I had doubts and struggled at times. Climb your way out of doubt using the staircase. Faith as the evidence of things unseen means that you trust the outcome will be manifest for your good. Even though you have a goal in mind, you have to have faith that the stairway is leading you toward your goal, which is an unseen future event. You have to remain open to the notion that accomplishing your goal may not be packaged in the way you envisioned.

The positivity treads help you frame the outcome for good no matter what it is, because you know and believe that all things work together for your good.

POSITIVITY PRACTICE

Climb Your Life Staircase

1. Meditate on what your Life Staircase looks like.

2. Draw it. Is it narrow and winding or wide and fabulous? What is on the landings?

3. Reflect on experiences when the staircase was steep, but you lifted your leg, and exercised your faith anyway.

4. Reflect on experiences when the steps brought you to a landing, place of rest, or pause before starting the climb.

5. Sit for 10 minutes every day, list the experiences during the day, and see which HOP you stepped on and how that encouraged you to keep stepping.

TRANSFORMATION

Reflect on the differences between when you did not step on your Life Staircase with faith versus how you feel now that you are laying down your HOP one tread at a time. Journal your responses below:

Before I started thinking about my Life Staircase as treads of positivity, I used to feel:

Now that I practice daily using the Habits of Positivity as the treads of my Life Staircase, I feel:

Journey to Healing

"This is the day that the Lord has made and I will rejoice and be glad in it."

—PSALM 118:24

> *"Your story is what you have, what you will always have. It is something to own."*
>
> **—MICHELLE OBAMA**

I BROKE TO THE SURFACE, gasping for air. My dream had pulled me into the depths of a seemingly bottomless ocean, with the weight of my subconscious pressing me deeper. Then suddenly, as if by magic, I was released and rocketed to the surface.

This was how I awakened on May 2, 2021, the 15th anniversary of the loss of our son, Matthew, at 24 weeks. For the first time ever, I turned to Charles, shared the disturbing dream, and we talked about our feelings surrounding that loss. I felt tormented in the dream because I was wrestling with whether there was something that I could have done to prevent Matthew's death. If you have a child, do you remember a class project where your child had to care for an egg at home for a period of time? In my dream, I dropped the egg, shattering the precious life, and I was devastated. However, as I emerged from under the weight of a massive column of water, talking to Charles about the dream restored my breath. When he shared that he had wrestled with similar feelings, it felt as if our relationship transformed at that moment.

I was incredulous that in the 15 years since Matthew's loss, we had never had that conversation. I had close girlfriends with whom I would share my sadness, but Charles never spoke of our loss. It was as if broaching the topic threatened to create an emotional flood that would sweep him away. In my sister circle, I would tentatively dip my toe into the water of the emotional ocean related to losing Matthew. As my body gradually adjusted to the temperature of the water, I could wade into those feelings and not get sucked under.

On the other hand, Charles had gone far inland, denying the very existence of the ocean. This was odd because the Charles I first met loved the ocean and would talk incessantly about his feelings. This journey of sharing our story had brought Charles back to the ocean where healing starts. I could feel the weight of all the years of buried emotions dissolve to reveal the beauty of the ocean. We were reminded why we love being on the Island of Positivity, where we are never far from the ocean. Together we could begin to release limiting beliefs that had kept us from our emotional ocean and embrace those feelings, which brought us into a deeper dimension of our relationship.

I have come full circle to where this book began — the healing power of story. When we apply a process that allows us to extract the positives from our stories, we open the floodgates of healing. As I wrote and cried and cried and wrote, a question that kept playing in my head was, "How did Charles feel?" I realized that we had never really talked about so many details of our infertility journey. I wanted him to share in this healing experience.

When couples are faced with difficult situations, there is often one partner who wants to stay strong for the other. There may not be space for them to express how they are dealing during the experience. I knew that, as the man, Charles was focused on being steadfast and strong for me, so when I asked him to share how he experienced those years, I had no idea that he was still so raw. It took him over a year to entertain digging into the trench where he had buried his pain and talk with me about it. We thought we had been through the trauma together, but in actuality, we were siloed in our coping. This process of discovery and sharing opened a common healing path for both of us and elevated our marriage to another level. The experience has been astounding.

When I first asked Charles to reflect on his feelings to add to the book, he said, "Absolutely not. I am not your target audience. Men don't focus on healing." He continued, "Men deal with the issue in real-time and move on. We don't talk about feelings." Oh my! I had never thought of my overly analytical, non-stop talking husband as being someone who would not share how he felt. Now that I look back, I recognize a clear transition point where he stopped talking about feelings related to this difficult and heartbreaking time. We had talked about all things tactical and logistical during the process. I remember that he was the one who called our family, friends and work colleagues whenever there was bad news to be delivered. I would shut down and crawl into bed, and he would be stoic and hold it together for both of us. What was so interesting was that once we started talking, it was as if I had turned on a faucet; he wouldn't stop talking!

My husband's hypothesis is that men bury the details of painful situations and ignore their feelings. The feelings become like a soda vigorously shaken in a can. When the can is opened, the result is explosive, with feelings spraying everywhere. Often, the details have been buried for so long that they become disassociated from the feelings, and then one doesn't even know where the feelings come from.

When Charles got the call that I had fainted in the operating room, he felt intense fear and concern for me. He could not remember anything other than the sickening, almost paralyzing fear. It was as if time stood still in his mind until he finally saw me hours later in the emergency room. I was stable, the pain had decreased, and I didn't look too bad. I was able to talk to him, and this alleviated some of his anxiety. However, his mind then took him on a journey to hopelessness, where he stopped believing or dreaming that this was ever going to happen. As he waited for the doctor after my surgery, he felt it would have been a relief if the doctor said we should stop trying. Then he could just put the entire thing behind him and not have to deal with the recurrent pain of disappointment and loss. He could even convince himself that this was not something that was extremely important to him. He was tired and worn out. As a defense mechanism, he limited himself and stopped emotionally investing in the dream. This allowed him to disconnect from the pain. The one thing that he knew with certainty was that he did not want to risk losing me. The roller coaster was too much. It felt easier not to be positive. It is simpler to take the easy way out and say this is not going to happen. It's more difficult to look an obstacle in the face and say, "Not today, negativity." In retrospect, he really wished that he had the Habits of Positivity at that time!

Charles was struck that, despite me being pounded both physically and emotionally, I did not stop believing that there would be a solution. After that episode with the ruptured ectopic pregnancy, we went back to the drawing board and untied the problem to identify areas on how we could approach this differently. We switched doctors, and I had fibroid surgery. I was Charles' gauge. As long as I was continuing to press forward, he would keep pace with me.

After the removal of 33 fibroids, we conceived by IVF. Charles was even more terrified, as he knew that being pregnant with twins could be fraught with complications for mother and babies. He could not share that fear with me. He could not share it with anyone, but as a neonatologist, he knew the risks. So, Charles carried that anxiety alone.

The day that we lost Matthew, Charles had a weird feeling that something was wrong. He was in a place of always waiting for the other shoe to drop because of the trauma that he had experienced with our multiple prior losses. After Matthew died, Charles was on pins and needles until we got to 28 weeks, and then he could exhale because he knew that even if Mark delivered early, he would likely be okay. However, he struggled with the fear related to my well-being. The statistics supported his concerns but the fact that I was so focused on Mark made him feel better.

When Mark and Matthew were born, Charles was relieved. He knew what to expect and how to take care of a baby born at 32 weeks. Even though I did not have the psychological capacity to hold Matthew, Charles held him for both of us. Amid the joy at the live birth of Mark and unspeakable grief as he viewed the perfectly formed body of our deceased son, Matthew, Charles stood, solid as a rock. He kissed Matthew, honored him and thanked him for being the angel that kept Mark in my uterus for as long as he did. The priest, called to the delivery room for this painful moment, baptized him, Matthew Charles Anderson. Charles described the look on Matthew's face as angelic, with a look of contentment that said he had fulfilled his purpose. Heaven's doors opened wide to welcome him.

So many couples and families that experience this type of trauma are so battered that they give up. Charles had the first-hand witness of families in the NICU whose marriages ended in divorce after the stress of their experience. I was relieved to discover statistics that couples who lose a child are not more likely to get divorced. Somehow, the shared journey of pain generates resilience. Within the limits of the pain lay the opportunity for a closer and deeper relationship and dependence on God. Miracles happen when we live our lives in dependence on God, which is what Charles and I have sought always to do.

One of the things that Charles said kept him going was the fact that I never gave up. I kept believing that having a child was possible, and I kept looking for solutions. I kept holding onto the positives and letting go of the negatives. Even in our lengthy process, I kept caring for others and serving. I kept finding those places of joy and gratitude. For those reasons, Charles held on and kept going. As we sat and reflected on our journey 20 years later, we stumbled upon the old unrevealed pain that needed to be exposed so that healing could begin. Our story possessed what we needed to heal. We had to start telling it. In order to tell it, we had to face it and extract the power in it. As I described in earlier chapters, we were able to embrace the positives even during the pain. The final step was healing.

We have taken the very journey that we are inviting you on. The healing power of our stories is real. How we extract meaning from our stories determines how they make a difference for you and others. Many themes surfaced in this book that speak to emotional, mental and physical health. Some of these issues were coronary artery disease, hypertension, infertility, loss of loved ones, prostate cancer, health disparities, increased infant and maternal mortality for Black women, COVID-19, toxic relationships and abuse, physician burnout, medical errors, sexual dysfunction, and intimacy. My gift to you is how to create a path to wholeness by using these experiences to build awareness and position you to be active, empowered, and positive along your journey.

The journey of building a positive mindset is a daily walk. Believe me, I have to constantly practice what I preach by accessing my internal Island of Positivity. This is the place where I could seek respite to redefine, recharge, reset and resume. I have to use my Habits of Positivity to redefine how I see the challenges, especially during this pandemic. I recharge by embracing stillness, meditating regularly, praying, and reading and writing more frequently. I believe that after time to reset, I can resume, ready to complete the assignment aligned with my purpose! This keeps me encouraged and motivated because, ultimately, we have no control of the future. I have to choose to stay in the present, believing that "all things work together for good."

Positivity is a process. It is neither toxic nor unrealistic, and it is achievable as a framework with which we approach our lives. Thinking positively affects our emotional, mental, and physical health. It is a minute-by-minute choice that I make every day. You can do it, too! As women, we wear so many hats. Our identity is connected to our appearance, race, country of origin, profession, caretaking status, mothering, and so on. Because of how much we carry, we are easy prey for negativity to steal our sense of value and worth. I started writing a version of this book 15 years ago, and there were so many times when I beat myself up about the fact that it was taking so long, but each story was like a tread on the Life Staircase, bringing me into God's sovereign timing and purpose for this book. It is truly meant for such a time as this.

My prayer is that as you sat with each of the chapters and reflected on how you see yourself in them, you have given yourself permission to work through your stories and apply and practice the Habits of Positivity one at a time, so they become a part of your consciousness. I also hope you have recognized that negativity shows up in so many ways—as a villain, as a monster, as room-darkening shades, as a squatter, as moldy clothes in your closet, and as a balloon-popping pin. In each of these instances, negativity's goal is to impose its unwelcome presence, subtract and steal from you, and eventually destroy you. But you are empowered to identify negativity and declare that it will not prevail today!

I hope you used your unique creativity to create your version of your Inner S.U.P.E.R. hero, Treasure Chest, Life Fabric, Joy Tank, Life Pendulum, Life Scales, Life Slingshot, Positivity Champion, Positivity Window, and Life Staircase. They represent a tangible reminder on the days when you need backup troops to get rid of negativity. I hope you understand that your Island of Positivity exists within you, wherever you are, and that you always have access to take a pause there to redefine, recharge and reset before you resume. I hope that as you continue to practice your Habits of Positivity, your back is straighter, you will hold your head higher, your shoulders are more squared, and your mind is more resolute. You can declare with confidence, "Not today, negativity! Not today!" I sincerely hope you recognize that this ongoing process of applying positivity habits to your life serves as armor to create some measure of protection from stressors. These stressors keep us in fight-or-flight mode, weather our bodies, and erode our emotional, mental, and physical health.

Most of all, I hope you discovered that you can change the lens through which you view your stories by applying them to a Positivity Scaffold. This can connect you to the power of self-healing, which now positions you to take part in someone else's healing. Thank you for taking this journey with me and for your willingness to take part in learning to think more positively. Your transformation will be ongoing as you apply the Positivity Scaffolds to your life and reap the benefits of your emotional, intellectual, mental, and physical well-being. Now that you have mastered the method, I hope you will become a Positivity Catalyst and take the journey with me to have your children, or any young people with whom you interact, use these habits. We have the opportunity to create an environment and culture of positivity which is the first step in establishing a powerful ecosystem of learning. I also hope that you will carry these 5 Habits of Positivity into every space you enter and that it will create transformation for others in the same way that it has created transformation for you and me!

DAILY REFLECTIONS

Continue to practice the Habits of Positivity on your journey to coping, hoping, and being well during times of challenge. Consider the following everyday reflections and journal your responses:

- What positive things did you discover about yourself today?

- What problem did you found a solution for?

- What challenge or limit did you encounter? How did you convert it to an opportunity?

- What positives did you keep? Which negatives did you discard?

- How did you live out your purpose of caring for others?

- What are you thankful for?

- What do you believe for tomorrow?

Positively yours,

Dr. Oneeka Williams

Bibliography

Bloeser, Claudia, and Titus Stahl. "Hope." *The Stanford Encyclopedia of Philosophy*. Ed Edward N. Zalta. Spring 2017 Edition. <https://plato.stanford.edu/archives/spr2017/entries/hope/>.

Boehm, Julia K., and Laura D. Kubzansky. "The Heart's Content: The Association Between Positive Psychological Well-Being and Cardiovascular Health." *Psychological Bulletin*. 17 April 2012

Clear, James. "How Your Beliefs Can Sabotage Your Behavior." *jamesclear.com*.

11 February 2021 <jamesclear.com/fixed-mindset-vs-growth-mindset>.

Dweck, Carol. *Mindset: The New Psychology of Success*. New York: Ballantine Books, 2007.

Fredrickson, B.L. *The broaden-and-build theory of positive emotions.* Philosophical Transactions of the Royal Society of London. Series B: *Biological Sciences,* 359(1449), 1367-1377.

Fredrickson, Barbara. *Positivity: Discover the Upward Spiral That Will Change Your Life*. New York: Harmony Books, 2009.

Gardner, Benjamin, et al. "Making health habitual: The psychology of 'habit-formation' and general practice." *British Journal of General Practice* 62.605 (2012): 664-666.

Geronimus, AT. "The weathering hypothesis and the health of African-American women and infants: Evidence and speculations." *Ethnicity Disease* 2.3 (1992): 207–221.

Hanson, Rick. "The Five Essential Skills." *Rickhanson.net.* 2020.

<www.rickhanson.net/articles/essential-skills>.

Krisch, Joshua A. "What Happens When You Tell Kids They're Just Like Dad." *fatherly.com.* 18 Jan. 2019 <www.fatherly.com/health-science/nature-vs-nurture-child-development>.

Morin, Amy. *13 Things Mentally Strong People Don't Do: Take Back Your Power, Embrace Change, Face Your Fears, and Train Your Brain for Happiness and Success.* New York: William Morrow, 2014.

Ostir, Glenn V, et al. "Hypertension in Older Adults and the Role of Positive Emotions." *Psychosomatic Medicine* 68.5 (2006): 727-733.

Seligman, Martin EP. *Flourish: A Visionary New Understanding of Happiness and Well-Being.* New York: Free Press, 2011.

Vilhauer, Jennice. "3 Effective Visualization Techniques to Change Your Life." *psychologytoday.com.* 30 June 2018 <www.psychologytoday.com/us/blog/living-forward/201806/3-effective-visualization-techniques-change-your-life>.

Whelan, Christine. *The Big Picture: A Guide to Finding Your Purpose in Life.* West Conshohocken: Templeton Press, 2016.

About the Author

DR. ONEEKA WILLIAMS, award-winning author, educator, entrepreneur, healer, storyteller, urologic surgeon, and Positivity Catalyst, is the product of a science teacher mother and journalist father. Born and raised in Guyana and Barbados, she is on a mission to educate, elevate and empower and believes we can use the positive power of our stories to defeat negativity so we can achieve whole health, pursue our dreams, and live a life without limits. A graduate of Johns Hopkins University and Harvard Medical School, she has used her experiences and life philosophy as the catapult to impact the lives of her patients and community.

As a mentor and advocate of health equity, literacy, and science education, Dr. Oneeka focuses on creating conditions of positivity as part of an ecosystem of learning. This shapes what we think, which then affects what we do and applies in any environment. She authors a book series featuring super surgeon Dr. Dee Dee Dynamo (www.drdeedeedynamo.com), who lives on the Island of Positivity, to inspire girls toward a greater interest in science and increase representation in children's books. Her focus on positive habits quickly attracted parents and teachers, underscoring that adults also need help in overcoming negativity in their lives. This is her first book for adults.

Dr. Oneeka practices urologic surgery and lives in Newton, Massachusetts, with her husband, Dr. Charles Anderson and son, Mark.

Learn more at www.DrOneekaWilliams.com and www.myislandofpositivity.com.

Made in USA - North Chelmsford, MA
1290905_9780998304557
11.18.2021 0853